Professional
Software
Development

Professional Software Development

Shorter Schedules,
Higher Quality Products,
More Successful Projects,
Enhanced Careers

Steve McConnell

~

⋀ Addison-Wesley

Boston • San Francisco • New York • Toronto • Montreal
London • Munich • Paris • Madrid
Capetown • Sydney • Tokyo • Singapore • Mexico City

The publisher offers discounts on this book when ordered in quantity for bulk purchases and special sales. For more information, please contact:

U.S. Corporate and Government Sales
(800) 382-3419
corpsales@pearsontechgroup.com

For sales outside of the U.S., please contact:

International Sales
(317) 581-3793
international@pearsontechgroup.com

Visit Addison-Wesley on the Web: www.awprofessional.com

Library of Congress Cataloging-in-Publication Data
McConnell, Steve.
    Professional software development : shorter schedules, higher quality products, more successful projects, enhanced careers / Steve McConnell.
        p.   cm.
    Includes bibliographical references and index.
    ISBN 0-321-19367-9 (alk. paper)
    1. Computer software—Development.   I. Title.

QA76.76.D47M392 2003
005.1—dc21

2003049596

ISBN: 0-321-19367-9
Text printed on recycled paper
1 2 3 4 5 6 7 8 9 10—CRS—0706050403
First printing, June 2003

All rising to a great place is by a winding stair.
FRANCIS BACON

*Success is the ability to go from one failure to another
with no loss of enthusiasm.*
WINSTON CHURCHILL

Contents

PART TWO
Individual Professionalism

PART THREE

Organizational Professionalism

PART FOUR

Industry Professionalism

Acknowledgments

I would like to thank the people who commented on major sections of the book including Don Bagert, Jon Bentley, Steven Black, Robert C. Burns (The Boeing Company), Trevor Burridge, Augusto Coppola, Alan B. Corwin (Process Builder), Ryan Fleming, Pat Forman, Robert L. Glass (Computing Trends), David Goodman, Owain E Griffiths, Bradey Honsinger, Larry M. Hughes (Sprint), Robert E. Lee, Avonelle Lovhaug, Mike Lutz, Steve Mattingly, Grant McLaughlin, Brian P. McLean, Hank Meuret, J. Fernando Naveda, Anthon Pang, David L. Parnas, Matt Peloquin, Tom Reed, Kathy Rhode, Steve Rinn, Wm. Paul Rogers, Jay Silverman, André Sintzoff, Tim Starry, Steve Tockey, Leonard L. Tripp, Tom Ventser (DMR Consulting Group), Karl Wiegers, and Greg Wilson.

Thanks also to the numerous reviewers who commented on specific topics.

Special thanks to the outstanding book production team at Addison-Wesley including Mike Hendrickson, Rebecca Greenberg, Amy Fleischer, Karin Hansen, and Janis Owens. It was a pleasure to work with each of them, and this book is much improved as a result of their contributions.

I also value my experience producing the first edition of this book, *After the Gold Rush*. I would like to remember the great work of Victoria Thulman, project editor, and the rest of the publication staff including Ben Ryan, Rob Nance, Cheryl Penner, and Paula Gorelick.

Introduction

It looks obvious until you try it.
IEEE SOFTWARE[1]

My flight was waiting on the runway when the captain made an announcement. "We've had some trouble with the plane's air conditioning system. In a plane, the air conditioner controls the oxygen levels so we need to make sure it's working before we can take off. Restarting the air conditioning unit hasn't worked, so we're going to power down the aircraft and power it back on. *These modern airplanes are all computer controlled, you know, so they're not very reliable.*"

The pilot powered down the airplane, powered it back up—essentially, rebooted the airplane—and our flight continued without incident. Needless to say, I was especially glad to deplane at the end of that particular trip.

The Best of Times, the Worst of Times

The best software organizations control their projects to meet defined quality targets. They accurately predict software delivery dates months or years in advance. They deliver their software projects within budget, and their productivity is constantly improving. Their staff morale is high, and their customers are highly satisfied.

- A telecom company needed to change about 3,000 lines of code in a code base of about 1 million lines of code. They made their changes so carefully that a year later no errors had been found in operation.

Their total time to make the changes—including requirements analysis, design, construction, and testing—was *9 hours*.[2]

- A team developing software for the United States Air Force committed to a one-year schedule and a $2 million budget even though other credible bids for the project had run as high as two years and $10 million. When the team delivered the project one month early, the project manager said the team's success arose from using techniques that have been known for years but that are rarely used in practice.[3]

- An aerospace company develops software for companies on a fixed-price basis. Three percent of its projects overrun their budgets; ninety-seven out of a hundred meet their targets.[4]

- An organization that committed to achieving outstanding quality attained an average of 39 percent reduction in its post-release defect rate every year for a period of 9 years—a cumulative reduction of 99 percent.[5]

In addition to these notable successes, software pumps billions of dollars into the economy every year, both directly through sales of software itself and indirectly through improved efficiency and through creation of products and services that are made possible only with software's support.

The practices needed to create good software have been well established and readily available for 10 to 20 years or more. Despite some amazing triumphs, however, the software industry is not living up to its full potential. There is a wide gulf between the average practice and the best, and many of the practices in widespread use are seriously outdated and underpowered. Performance of the average software project leaves much to be desired, as many well-known disasters will attest.

- The IRS bumbled an $8 billion software modernization program that cost the United States taxpayers $50 billion per year in lost revenue.[6]

- The FAA's Advanced Automation System overran its planned budget by about $3 billion.[7]

- Problems with the baggage handling system caused a delay of more than a year in opening Denver International Airport. Estimates of the delay's cost ranged as high as $1.1 million per day.[8]

- The Ariane 5 rocket blew up on its maiden launch because of a software error.[9]
- The B-2 bomber wouldn't fly on its maiden flight because of a software problem.[10]
- Computer-controlled ferries in Seattle caused more than a dozen dock crashes, resulting in damage worth more than $7 million. The state of Washington recommended spending more than $3 million to change the ferries back to manual controls.[11]

Many projects that are lower profile than these are equally troubled. Roughly 25 percent of all projects fail outright,[12] and the typical project is 100 percent over budget at the point it's cancelled. Fifty percent of projects are delivered late, over budget, or with less functionality than desired.[13]

At the company level, these cancelled projects represent tremendous lost opportunity. If projects that are ultimately cancelled could be shut down at 10 percent of their intended budgets rather than 200 percent, imagine what a company could do by redirecting those resources at projects that were not ultimately cancelled.

At the national level, cancelled projects represent prodigious economic waste. A rough calculation suggests that cancelled software projects currently impose about a $40 billion drain on the United States economy.[14]

When projects succeed, they can still present risks to the public safety or welfare. A project lead at Lotus received a call from a surgeon who was using a spreadsheet to analyze patient data during open-heart surgery.[15] *Newsweek* magazine printed pictures of soldiers using Microsoft Excel on laptop computers to plan operations, and the Excel technical support team has received calls from the battlefield during active military operations.

The Purpose of This Book

Software development can be predictable, controllable, economical, and manageable. Software isn't usually developed that way, but it can be developed that way. This book is about the emerging profession of software engineering—and professional software practices that support economical creation of high-quality software.

The essays in this book address questions like these:

- What is software engineering?
- How does software engineering relate to computer science?
- Why isn't regular computer programming good enough?
- Why do we need a *profession* of software engineering?
- Why is *engineering* the best model for a software development profession?
- In what ways do effective practices vary from project to project (or company to company), and in what ways are they usually the same?
- What can organizations do to support a professional approach to software development?
- What can individual software developers do to become full-fledged professionals?
- What can the software industry as a whole do to create a true profession of software engineering?

How This Book Is Organized

The parts in this book progress from looking at the trade of computer programming as it exists today to exploring the profession of software engineering as it might exist in the future.

Part 1, The Software Tar Pit, explains how the software field got to be the way it is. There are many valid reasons why the software field came to its current state. Understanding those reasons should be used to accelerate, not delay, the changes needed to make successful projects an everyday habit.

Part 2, Individual Professionalism, looks at the steps individuals can take on their own to achieve higher levels of software professionalism.

Software projects are so complex that numerous key factors cannot be addressed effectively at the individual level. Part 3, Organizational Professionalism, digs into the organizational practices needed to support more professional software projects.

Part 4, Industry Professionalism, examines steps that must be taken by the software industry at large to support professionalism at the individual and organizational levels.

What I've Learned Since 1999

Professional Software Development is an updated and significantly expanded edition of my 1999 book, *After the Gold Rush*.[16] Since 1999, I've learned several lessons that are reflected in this new edition:

- Licensing of software developers is more controversial than I expected. I still think that licensing a small percentage of software engineers is an important step toward protecting the general public's safety and welfare. I have tried to clarify that licensing is only one of many initiatives needed to improve the software development profession, and not the most important one.

- Education of software engineers does not have to be tightly linked to licensing. Undergraduate and graduate educational programs can seek to instill an engineering mindset in software developers without necessarily preparing them to become licensed professional engineers. Indeed, if fewer than five percent of software developers are eventually licensed—which seems likely—targeting the majority of educational programs at licensing seems misguided.

- The world didn't fall apart on January 1, 2000. Although I didn't think Y2K would be catastrophic, I did believe that Y2K-related problems would be more significant than they were. The software industry's repair efforts turned out to be far more effective than I expected. Beyond that, the Y2K problem itself was in some sense a result of *successful* software development practices. Y2K would not have been an issue in the first place if so many software systems had not survived longer than their originally expected lifespans.

- Modern software development is truly impressive in many respects, and any comments about professionalizing the field of software development should account for software's numerous successes. We must be careful not to throw out the field's better practices as we try to strengthen the weaker ones.

Who Should Read This Book

If you develop software for a living, this book will explore what you need to do to become a truly professional software developer.

If you manage software projects, this book will summarize the differences between poorly run and well run software projects and overview what you can do to make your projects more successful.

If you manage a software organization, this book will outline the benefits available from systematic approaches to software development and sketch what you need to do to realize those benefits.

If you are a student who wants to work in the software field, this book will introduce you to the body of knowledge that makes up the field of software engineering and show you what a career in software engineering will look like.

Toward Professional Software Development

Industry researchers have long observed 10 to 1 differences in productivity between different organizations competing in the same industries.[17] More recently, researchers have observed differences as high as 600 to 1.[18] The most effective organizations are doing very well indeed.

The benefits of creating a true profession of software engineering are compelling. Traditional thinking would have it that change presents the greatest risk. In software's case, the greatest risk lies with not changing—staying mired in unhealthy, extravagant development practices instead of switching to practices that were proven to be more effective many years ago.

How to change? That is the central topic of the rest of this book.

—Bellevue, Washington

Memorial Day, 2003

Notes

1. This is from a book review in *IEEE Software* about the book *Software Engineering Principles and Practice* by Hans van Vliet, West Sussex, England: John Wiley & Sons Ltd, 1993.

2. Pitterman, Bill, "Telcordia Technologies: The Journey to High Maturity," *IEEE Software,* July 2000.

3. Gibbs, W. Wayt, "Command and Control: Inside a Hollowed-Out Mountain, Software Fiascoes—and a Signal Success," *Scientific American,* August 1997, pp. 33–34. Tackett, Buford D., III, and Buddy Van Doren, "Process Control for Error Free Software: A Software Success Story," *IEEE Software,* May 1999.

4. Private communication with the author.

5. Herbsleb, James, et al., *Benefits of CMM Based Software Process Improvement: Initial Results,* Pittsburgh: Software Engineering Institute, Document CMU/SEI-94-TR-13, August 1994.

6. Anthes, Gary H., "IRS Project Failures Cost Taxpayers $50B Annually," *Computerworld,* October 14, 1996.

7. Britcher, Robert N., "Why (Some) Large Computer Projects Fail," in Glass, Robert L., *Software Runaways,* Englewood Cliffs, NJ: Prentice Hall, 1998. Gibbs, W. Wayt, "Software's Chronic Crisis," *Scientific American,* September 1994, pp. 86–95.

8. Glass, Robert L., *Software Runaways,* Englewood Cliffs, NJ: Prentice Hall, 1998. Gibbs, W. Wayt, "Software's Chronic Crisis," *Scientific American,* September 1994, pp. 86–95.

9. Nuseibeh, Bashar, "Ariane 5: Who Dunnit?" *IEEE Software,* May/June 1997, pp. 15–16.

10. Fishman, Charles, "They Write the Right Stuff," *Fast Company,* December 1996.

11. Neumann, Peter G., *Computer Related Risks,* Reading, MA: Addison-Wesley, 1995.

12. The Standish Group, "Charting the Seas of Information Technology," Dennis, MA: The Standish Group, 1994. Jones, Capers, *Patterns of Software Systems Failure and Success,* Boston, MA: International Thomson Computer Press, 1996.

13. The Standish Group, "Charting the Seas of Information Technology," Dennis, MA: The Standish Group, 1994.

14. This rough calculation is based on the employment figures presented in Table 7-2, "Job breakdown for software workers," on the job titles of computer and information scientists, research; computer programmers; computer software engineers, applications; computer software engineers, systems software; and computer systems analysts. Other job titles were not considered in this analysis. Total U.S. economic expenditure on software development was computed by multiplying an average fully burdened labor cost of $95,000 times 1,741,000 personnel in the job titles listed. Of the total amount of roughly $160 billion, 25% is the amount that is spent on cancelled projects. This analysis may understate the impact of cancelled projects due to the fact that the risk of cancellation increases with the size of the project, so that cancelled projects may be more costly than average projects.

15. Wiener, Lauren Ruth, *Digital Woes: Why We Should Not Depend on Software,* Reading, MA: Addison-Wesley, 1993.

16. McConnell, Steve, *After the Gold Rush,* Redmond, WA: Microsoft Press, 1999.

17. Mills, Harlan D., *Software Productivity,* Boston, MA: Little, Brown, 1983.

18. Yourdon, Edward, *Rise and Resurrection of the American Programmer,* Englewood Cliffs, NJ: Prentice Hall, 1996.

PART ONE

The Software Tar Pit

CHAPTER ONE

Wrestling with Dinosaurs

He that will not apply new remedies must expect new evils,
for time is the greatest innovator.

FRANCIS BACON

In 1975, Fred Brooks compared the development of large software systems to dinosaurs, woolly mammoths, and saber-toothed tigers fighting the glutinous grip of the tar pit.[1]* Brooks predicted that the software engineering tar pit would continue to be sticky for a long time to come.

The problems that Brooks described more than twenty-five years ago were not new when he described them, and the software community has now had another quarter century to work on them. How much progress has been made?

Many of the problems plaguing the typical software project today haven't changed much. For example, schedule pressure is a common feature of today's projects. According to some estimates, excessive schedule pressure occurs in about 75 percent of all medium-sized projects and in 90 percent or more of all large projects.[2] Overtime is more the norm than the exception.[3] Modern startup companies are known for the long hours they expect from their employees and stories of programmers sleeping under their desks abound,[4] but as long ago as the mid-1960s one report stated that, "In many companies, programmers faced with deadlines have been known to spend nights in the offices."[5] In 1975, Fred Brooks pointed out

---

*Citations for data cited and further reading can be found in the Notes section at the end of each chapter.

that "more software projects have gone awry for lack of calendar time than all other causes combined."[6] Schedule overruns have been around for at least 30 years and—people's impatience being what it is—probably since time immemorial.

The scope of today's large software projects seems daunting, and a natural tendency is to think that no one ever attempted projects of the scope we now face. Yet even a huge project such as the development of Windows NT has historical precedents. The initial Windows NT project required about 1,500 staff-years of effort,[7] but the development of IBM's OS/360, which was completed in 1966, required more than three times as much effort.[8]

Recent surveys have found that the most frequent causes of software project failure have to do with requirements problems—requirements that define the wrong system, that are too ambiguous to support detailed implementation, or that change frequently and wreak havoc on the system design.[9] But requirements problems are not new. Back in 1969, Robert Frosch observed that a system could "satisfy the letter of the specification and still not be very satisfactory."[10]

Modern developers rack their brains trying to keep up with the frenetic pace of change brought on by Web development. How do you keep up with new languages, shifting standards, and vendors that release new products every few months? To those of us who have been in the industry for a couple of decades, this sounds an awful lot like the mid-1980s when the IBM PC began to revolutionize corporate computing.

When the Fortran programming language was developed in 1954–58, it was supposed to eliminate the need for computer programming—scientists and engineers could simply enter their formulas into the computer, and the computer would translate the formulas for them, thus the name FORmula TRANslation. Of course, Fortran didn't eliminate programming; it just reduced the need for machine-language programming. From time to time we still hear about the promise of automatic programming.[11] Computers will become so advanced that the need for computer programmers will disappear. But this was already a well-worn chestnut more than thirty-five years ago when Gene Bylinsky reported that, "Predictions of businessmen blithely conversing with their omnipotent machines in plain English still get played up regularly in the press."[12] The reality is that defining problems in painstaking detail is difficult work. That aspect of computer programming will not go away. New tools are useful, but not a substitute for clear thinking. I made that point in my 1996 book *Rapid Development,* but Robert Frosch had already made the same point in *IEEE Spectrum* 30 years earlier.

Internet developers talk about development in Internet time. The Internet makes it possible for developers to roll out revisions to their programs with ease. Users can download upgrades electronically, without requiring duplication of CDs or DVDs, which makes delivery of upgrades quick and inexpensive. This contributes to pressure to release upgrades frequently in response to user requests. Internet developers say that users would rather get the software quickly than have it be perfect. Internet developers sometimes say, "It's better to be first than right."

How unprecedented is this really? Some Internet developers think these dynamics are unique to Web projects, but industry old-timers know better: low rollout cost, easy corrections, low cost of failure—this sounds like a good old-fashioned in-house mainframe production environment.

These common threads tying together 25 years of software development are a source of both comfort and despair. The despair arises from the fact that some problems have been with us for a quarter century or more and are still common. We truly have been stuck in the tar pit a long time. The comfort arises from the same source: we've been staring at the same problems long enough to recognize the patterns, and—as I intend to explore throughout the rest of this book—we seem to be the brink of fixing them.

Notes

1. Brooks, Frederick P., Jr., *The Mythical Man-Month,* Anniversary Edition, Reading, MA: Addison-Wesley, 1995. The original edition was published in 1975.

2. Data on frequency of schedule pressure comes from Capers Jones, *Assessment and Control of Software Risks,* Englewood Cliffs, NJ: Yourdon Press, 1994. For information on common schedule performance, see The Standish Group, "Charting the Seas of Information Technology," Dennis, MA: The Standish Group, 1994; and

Capers Jones, *Patterns of Software Systems Failure and Success,* Boston, MA: International Thomson Computer Press, 1996.

3. I discuss this in detail in *Rapid Development* (Redmond, WA: Microsoft Press, 1996).

4. Bronson, Po, "Manager's Journal," *Wall Street Journal,* February 9, 1998.

5. Bylinsky, Gene, "Help Wanted: 50,000 Programmers," *Fortune,* March 1967, pp. 141ff.

6. Brooks, Frederick P., Jr., *The Mythical Man-Month,* Reading, MA: Addison-Wesley, 1975.

7. This number is estimated. It is based on the reported cost for Windows NT being $150 million (Zachary, Pascal, *Showstopper! The Breakneck Race to Create Windows NT and the Next Generation at Microsoft,* New York: Free Press, 1994) and a fully burdened labor cost of $100,000/staff-year.

8. Effort was approximately 5,000 staff months. Brooks, Frederick P., Jr., *The Mythical Man-Month,* Reading, MA: Addison-Wesley, 1975.

9. Cole, Andy, "Runaway Projects—Cause and Effects," *Software World,* Vol. 26, no. 3, pp. 3–5. The Standish Group, "Charting the Seas of Information Technology," Dennis, MA: The Standish Group, 1994.

10. Frosch, Robert A., "A New Look at Systems Engineering," *IEEE Spectrum,* September 1969.

11. Rich, Charles, and Richard C. Waters, "Automatic Programming: Myths and Prospects," *IEEE Computer,* August 1988.

12. Bylinsky, Gene, "Help Wanted: 50,000 Programmers," *Fortune,* March 1967, pp. 141ff.

CHAPTER TWO

Fool's Gold

Hope is a good breakfast, but it is a bad supper.
FRANCIS BACON

Software problems have persisted partly because of the bewitching appeal of a few common, ineffective practices. During the California Gold Rush in the late 1840s and early 50s, some prospectors were deceived by fool's gold—iron pyrite—a substance that has the luster and sparkle of gold. Unlike gold, iron pyrite is flaky, brittle, and virtually valueless. Experienced miners know that real gold is soft, malleable, and doesn't break under pressure. For 50 years, software developers have been succumbing to the temptation of their own fool's gold. They are drawn to flawed practices that have a seductive appeal, but the practices that make up software's fool's gold, like iron pyrite, are flaky, brittle, and virtually valueless.

Moving the Block

Looking back many centuries before the California Gold Rush, suppose that you were working on one of the ancient pyramids and were given the assignment to move an enormous stone block 10,000 meters from a river to the site of a pyramid under construction, as shown in Figure 2-1. You are given 100 days to move the block and 20 people with which to move it.

You are allowed to use any method you like to get it to its destination. Each day, you have to move the block an average of 100 meters closer to the pyramid, or you have to do something that will reduce the number of days needed to travel the remaining distance.

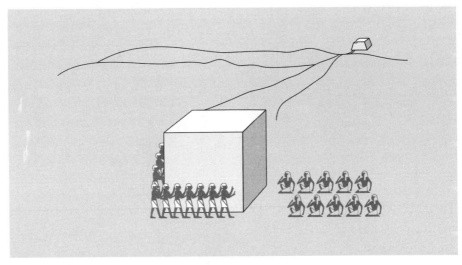

FIGURE 2-1

One way to think of a software project is as a heavy block of stone. You must either move the block one day closer to the final destination each day, or you must do something that will enable you to traverse the remaining distance in one less day.

Some block-moving teams might immediately begin pushing the block, trying to move it with brute force. With a very small block, this method might work, but with a heavy block resting directly on desert sand, this approach won't move the block very quickly, if at all. If the block moves ten meters per day, the fact that it is moving at all might be satisfying, but the team is actually falling 90 meters per day behind. "Progress" doesn't necessarily mean sufficient progress.

The smart block-moving team wouldn't jump straight into trying to move the block with brute force. They know that for all but the smallest blocks, they will need to spend time planning how to move the block before they put their muscles into it. After analyzing their assignment, they might decide to cut down a few trees and use the tree trunks as rollers, as shown in Figure 2-2. That will take a day or two, but chances are good that it will increase the speed at which they can move the block.

What if trees aren't readily available, and the team has to spend several days hiking up river to find any trees? The hike is still probably a good

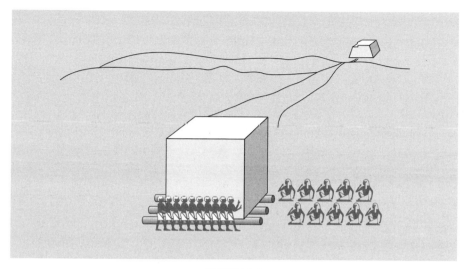

FIGURE 2-2

Whether moving a block of stone or creating computer software, the smart team takes time at the beginning of the project to plan its work so that it can work quickly and efficiently.

investment, especially since the team that begins by trying to use brute force will only move the block a fraction of the distance needed each day.

Similarly, the smart block-moving team might want to prepare the surface over which they'll be moving the block. Instead of pushing it across the sand, they might want to create a level roadway first, which will be an especially good idea if they have more than just this one block to move.

A really sophisticated block-moving team might start with the roller and road system, and eventually realize that having only the minimum number of rollers available forces them to stop work too often; they have to move the back roller to the front of the block every time they move the block forward one roller-width. By having a few extra rollers on hand and assigning some people to move the rollers from back to front, they're better able to maintain their momentum.

They might also realize that their pushing is limited by how many people can fit around the block's base. They might create a harness so that they can pull the block from the front at the same time they're pushing it

FIGURE 2-3
Smart teams continuously look for ways to work more efficiently.

from behind, as illustrated in Figure 2-3. As more people divide the work, they find that each person's work is easier, and the faster pace is actually more sustainable than the slower one.

Stone Blocks and Software

How does this block moving relate to software? The movement of the stone block is analogous to creating source code. If you have 100 days to complete a software project, you either need to complete 1/100 of the source code each day, or you need to do work that will allow you to complete the remaining source code faster. Because the work of creating source code is much less tangible than the work of moving a stone block, progress at the beginning of a software project can be harder to gauge. Software projects are vulnerable to a "last minute syndrome" in which the project team has little sense of urgency at the beginning of a project, fritters away days on end, and works itself into a desperate frenzy by the end of the project. Thinking of a project's source code as a stone block makes it clear that you can't hope to conduct a successful project by sprinting at the end. Every day, a software project manager should ask, "Did we move the block one day closer to our destination today? If not, did we reduce our remaining work by one day?"

Another way that moving a stone block relates to software is that, eventually, no matter how much planning you do, you do have to move the block; you do have to write the source code. Source-code creation on all but the smallest projects involves an enormous amount of detail work, and it's easy to underestimate it.

Code-and-Fix Development

The problem of not focusing enough on making rollers and preparing roadways is by far the most common problem in software. About 75 percent of the software project teams begin their projects by hurling themselves against the block and trying to move it with brute force.[1] This approach is called "code-and-fix development"—jumping straight into coding without planning or designing the software first. Sometimes teams do this because the team's software developers are anxious to begin coding. Sometimes they do it because managers or customers are eager to see tangible signs of progress. Code-and-fix development is universally ineffective on all but the tiniest projects.

The problem with the code-and-fix approach, as with the brute force approach to moving the stone block, is that quick movement off the starting line doesn't necessarily translate into quick progress toward the finish line. The team that uses a more advanced approach is putting a framework in place that will allow the project to spin up to a high level of productivity and finish efficiently. It is putting rollers under the block, clearing the roadway, and preparing to focus the energy of the project team. The code-and-fix project gets the block moving early, but it doesn't move the block far enough each day and the brute force approach isn't sustainable. It typically leads to the creation of hundreds or thousands of defects early in the project. Several studies have found that 40 to 80 percent of a typical software project's budget goes into fixing defects that were created earlier on the same project.[2]

Figure 2-4 illustrates the way that productivity erodes over time on a code-and-fix project. Little or no effort is put into planning and process management at the beginning of the project. Some small amount of effort goes into thrashing (unproductive work), but most work goes into coding. As the project moves forward, fixing defects becomes an increasingly prominent feature of the project. By the end of the project, the project that uses code-and-fix development is typically spending most of its time fixing the defects that it created earlier.

As Figure 2-4 suggests, the lucky code-and-fix projects are brought to completion while they are still eking out some small amount of coding

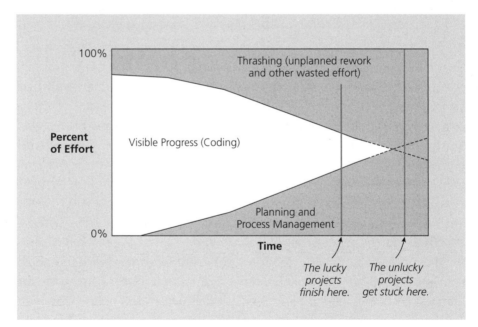

FIGURE 2-4

Using a code-and-fix approach, the lucky projects finish while they are still eking out a small amount of productive work. The unlucky projects get stuck in a zone where 100 percent of their effort is consumed by thrashing, planning, and process management.
Source: Adapted from *Software Project Survival Guide.*[3]

progress. The unlucky projects get stuck on the far right side of the diagram where 100 percent of their available effort is consumed by planning, process management, and thrashing, and they are not making any coding progress. Without enough up-front planning, the code quickly becomes flaky and brittle. Some of these projects might be rescued by taking steps to push the team back to the left enough that they can eke out a release. The remaining projects are eventually cancelled.

This gloomy picture is no exaggeration. Several studies have reported that about 25 percent of all software projects are eventually cancelled.[4] At the time the average project is cancelled, it's 100 percent over budget and is caught in an extended debug, test, and fix cycle (thrashing). The reason it's cancelled is the perception that its quality problems are insurmountable.[5]

The irony of this dynamic is that these unsuccessful projects eventually do as much planning and process management as a successful project would. They have to implement defect tracking to manage all the bugs being reported. They begin estimating more carefully as the release date approaches. Toward the end of the project, the project team might re-estimate as often as every week or even every day. They spend time managing expectations of project stakeholders, convincing them that the project will eventually be released. They may begin tracking defects and imposing standards for debugging code before it's integrated with already-debugged code. But because they begin these practices late in the project, the benefits from these practices are leveraged over only a small part of the project.

The kinds of practices they implement are different from the kinds a more effective organization would implement in a project's early stages. And many of the practices they implement wouldn't have been needed if the project had been run well from the beginning.

As Figure 2-5 illustrates, the most sophisticated organizations—those that produce the most reliable software for the least cost and with the shortest schedules—spend a relatively small percentage of their budgets on the construction part of a project. The least sophisticated organizations spend practically their whole budgets on coding and fixing bugs in their code. Their total budgets are much higher because they don't lay any groundwork for working efficiently. (I'll return to this dynamic in more detail in Chapter 14.)

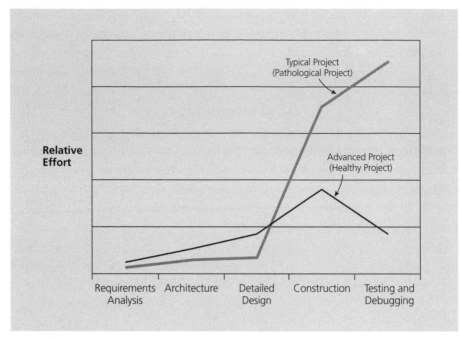

FIGURE 2-5

Advanced software development approaches require more work during the early stages of the project to eliminate an enormous amount of unnecessary work in the later stages of a project.[6]

Code-and-fix development continues to be used because it is appealing in two ways. First, it allows the project team to show signs of progress immediately—they can begin moving the stone block 10 meters per day the first day, while the more effective team is still out cutting down trees, preparing the roadway for a smooth trip, and showing no visible signs of progress on the real problem of moving the block. If managers and customers aren't very sophisticated about the dynamics of a successful project, a code-and-fix approach looks appealing. A second source of code-and-fix development's appeal is that it requires no training. In an industry in which the average level of software engineering training is low, it has been the most common method by default.

The code-and-fix approach is one form of software fool's gold. It seems attractive at first glance, but experienced software developers recognize it as having little value.

Focus on Quality

You might assume that a software project can be shortened by spending less time on testing or technical reviews. "Needless overhead!" say people with a taste for code-and-fix development. Industry experience indicates otherwise. An attempt to trade quality for cost or schedule actually results in increased cost and a longer schedule.

As Figure 2-6 illustrates, projects that remove about 95 percent of their defects prior to release are the most productive; they spend the least time

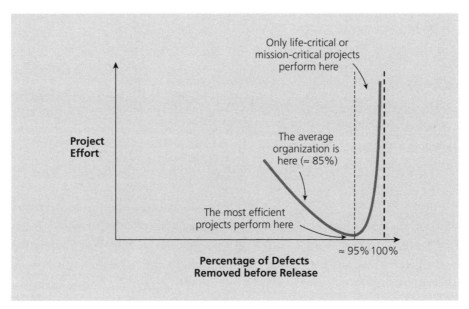

FIGURE 2-6
Up to a point, the projects that achieve the lowest defect rates also achieve the shortest schedules. Most projects can shorten their schedules by focusing on fixing defects earlier.
Source: Adapted from *Applied Software Measurement: Assuring Productivity and Quality,* 2d Ed.[7]

fixing their own defects. Beyond about 95 percent defect removal, projects have to expend extra effort to improve quality. Short of 95 percent, projects can become more efficient by removing more defects sooner. Approximately 75 percent of software projects presently fit into this category. For the projects in this category, the attempt to trade quality for cost or schedule is another example of fool's gold. It's also an example of a software project dynamic that isn't really new. IBM discovered 25 years ago that projects that focused their efforts on attaining the shortest schedules had high frequencies of cost and schedule overruns. Projects that focused on achieving low defect counts had the best schedules and the highest productivities.[8]

Some Fool's Gold Is Silver

Technologies and methodologies that are associated with extravagant productivity claims are called "silver bullets" because they are supposed to slay the werewolf of low productivity.[9] For decades, the software industry has been plagued by claims that the UmptyFratz Innovation dramatically improves development speed. In the 1960s, on-line programming was associated with this claim. In the 1970s, it was third-generation languages. In the 1980s, advocates for artificial intelligence and CASE tools made these promises. In the 1990s, object-oriented programming was lauded as the next great productivity boon. In the early 2000s, it was development in Internet time.

Suppose that a stone-block project team starts out using the brute-force method to move the stone block. After a few days, the team leader can see that progress isn't fast enough to meet the project's goals. Fortunately, he has heard of an amazing animal called an "elephant." Elephants can weigh almost 100 times as much as an adult human being and are extremely powerful. The project leader mounts an expedition to capture and bring back an elephant to help the team move the block. After a three-week safari, the team returns with a captive elephant. They harness the magnificent beast to the block and crack the whip. They hold their collective breath, waiting to see just how fast the elephant will move the block. They may even finish ahead of schedule! As they watch, the elephant begins pulling the block forward, much faster than the team of humans had ever been able to accomplish. But then, unexpectedly, the elephant rears on its hind legs. It breaks its harness, tramples two of its handlers, and runs off at 40 kilometers per hour, never to be seen again (as shown in Figure 2-7). The stone-block team is dejected. "Maybe we should have spent more time learning how to handle the elephant before we started using him on a real project," they thought. They wasted more than 20 percent of their schedule looking for the elephant, lost two of their teammates, and are no closer to the goal than when they started.

That, in a nutshell, is Silver Bullet Syndrome.

The elephant analogy is more apt than you might think. Robert L. Glass chronicles 16 troubled projects in *Software Runaways*.[10] Four of the projects he describes expected to be breakthrough successes because of their use of silver bullet innovations. Instead, they ended up failing because of the same innovations.

A special kind of silver bullet is forged from attempts to implement organizational process improvement half-heartedly. Some organizations try to implement organizational improvement with buzzwords—TQM, QFD,

FIGURE 2-7
Silver bullet innovations often fall short of expectations.

SW-CMM, Zero Defects, Six Sigma, Continuous Improvement, Statistical Process Control—these are all valuable practices when properly applied by focusing on the substance of the practice and not just the form. But each of these practices is virtually worthless when applied as buzzwords. Some organizations cycle through them in 12-month intervals, as if ritualistically chanting the initials of a current management fad could call forth improvements in quality and productivity. A special place in low-productivity hell is reserved for these organizations. After years of Management By Buzzword (MBB), entire staffs become cynical about organizational improvement initiatives in general, which adds one more challenge to escaping from code-and-fix development.

The right innovation applied to the right project, supported by appropriate training and deployed with realistic expectations can be tremendously beneficial as a long-term strategy. But new innovations aren't magic and they aren't easy. When they are adopted with a get-rich-quick attitude, innovations become fool's gold.

Software Isn't Soft

One more kind of fool's gold is the belief that software is soft. Hardware is "hard" because it is difficult to change. Software was originally called "soft" because it was easy to change. For very small programs at the dawn of computer programming, this might have been true. As software systems have become more complex, however, this notion that software is easy to change has become one of the most pernicious ideas in software development.

Several studies have found that changing requirements—attempts to take advantage of software's supposed softness—are the most common or one of the most common sources of cost and schedule overruns.[11] They are also a major factor in project cancellations; in some cases, changes resulting from creeping requirements can destabilize a product to such a degree that it can't be finished at all.[12]

A simple example illustrates why software isn't as soft as people think. Suppose that you are asked to design a system that will initially print a set of five reports and eventually print a set of 10 reports. You have several kinds of flexibility—softness—that you will need to be concerned about:

- Is ten an upper limit on the number of reports?
- Will the future reports be similar to the initial five reports?
- Will all of the reports always be printed?
- Will they always be printed in the same order?
- To what extent will the user be able to customize the reports?
- Will users be allowed to define their own reports?
- Will the reports be customizable and definable on the fly?
- Will the reports be translated to other languages?

No matter how carefully the software is designed, there will always be a point at which the software won't be soft. In the case of the reports, any of the following areas could turn out to be "hard":

- Defining more than ten reports
- Defining a new report that is different from the initial set of reports
- Printing a subset of the reports
- Printing the reports in a user-defined order
- Allowing the user to customize reports
- Allowing the user to define an entire custom report
- Translating the reports to another language that uses a Latin alphabet
- Translating the reports to another language that uses a non-Latin alphabet or that reads right to left

What's interesting about this example is that I can ask a whole hat full of questions about the "softness" of these reports without knowing anything whatsoever about the specific reports or even about the system within which the reports will be printed. Simply knowing that there are "some reports" raises many general questions about the different degrees of softness.

It's tempting to say that software developers should always design the software to be as flexible as possible, but flexibility is an almost infinitely variable entity, and it comes at a price. If the user really wants a standard set of five preformatted reports, always printed as a set, and always printed in the same order in the same language, the software developer should not create an elaborate utility that allows the user to generate highly customized reports. That could easily cost the customer 100 to 1,000 times as much as providing the basic functionality the user really needs. The user (or client or manager) has a responsibility to help software developers define the specific flexibility needed.

Flexibility costs money now. Limiting flexibility saves money now, but typically costs disproportionately more money later. The difficult engineering judgment is weighing the known present need against the possible future need and determining how "soft" or "hard" to make the "ware."

How Fool's Gold Pans Out

In conclusion, we hold the following software truths to be self-evident (or evident after careful examination, anyway):

- The success of a software project depends on not writing source code too early in the project.
- You can't trade defect count for cost or schedule unless you're working on life-critical systems. Focus on defect count; cost and schedule will follow.
- Silver bullets are hazardous to a project's health, though software industry history suggests that vendors will continue to claim otherwise.
- Half-hearted process improvement is an especially damaging kind of silver bullet because it undermines future improvement attempts.
- Despite its name, software isn't soft, unless it's made that way in the first place, and making it soft is expensive.

The software world has had 50 years to learn these lessons. The most successful people and organizations have taken them to heart. Learning to resist software's fool's gold consistently is one of the first steps the software industry needs to take on the road to creating a true profession of software engineering.

Notes

1. This average is based on the number of software projects at SW-CMM Level 1. See Chapter 14 for more details about this statistic.

2. Software Engineering Institute, quoted in Fishman, Charles, "They Write the Right Stuff," *Fast Company,* December 1996. Mills, Harlan D., *Software Productivity,* Boston, MA: Little, Brown, 1983, pp. 71–81. Wheeler, David, Bill Brykczynski, and Reginald Meeson, *Software Inspection: An Industry Best Practice,* Los Alamitos, CA: IEEE Computer Society Press, 1996. Jones, Capers, *Programming Productivity,* New York: McGraw-Hill, 1986. Boehm, Barry W., "Improving Software Productivity," *IEEE Computer,* September 1987, pp. 43–57.

3. McConnell, Steve, *Software Project Survival Guide,* Redmond, WA: Microsoft Press, 1997. This book contains a more in-depth description of these dynamics.

4. Johnson, Jim, "Turning Chaos into Success," *Software Magazine,* December 1999, pp. 30–39. The Standish Group, "Charting the Seas of Information Technology," Dennis, MA: The Standish Group, 1994. Jones, Capers, *Assessment and Control of Software Risks,* Englewood Cliffs, NJ: Yourdon Press, 1994.

5. Jones, Capers, *Assessment and Control of Software Risks,* Englewood Cliffs, NJ: Yourdon Press, 1994.

6. The "advanced project" profile is based on projects performed by NASA's Software Engineering Lab. The "typical project" is from project data I've compiled from my consulting work and is consistent with data reported by Capers Jones, *Patterns of Software Systems Failure and Success,* Boston, MA: International Thomson Computer Press, 1996, and other sources.

7. Jones, Capers, *Applied Software Measurement: Assuring Productivity and Quality,* 2d Ed., New York: McGraw-Hill, 1997.

8. Jones, Capers, *Programming Productivity,* New York: McGraw-Hill, 1986.

9. Brooks, Frederick P., Jr., "No Silver Bullets—Essence and Accidents of Software Engineering," *Computer,* April 1987, pp. 10–19.

10. Glass, Robert L., *Software Runaways,* Englewood Cliffs, NJ: Prentice Hall, 1998.

11. Vosburgh, J., B. Curtis, R. Wolverton, B. Albert, H. Malec, S. Hoben, and Y. Liu, "Productivity Factors and Programming Environments," *Proceedings of the 7th*

International Conference on Software Engineering, Los Alamitos, CA: IEEE Computer Society, 1984, pp. 143–152. Lederer, Albert L., and Jayesh Prasad, "Nine Management Guidelines for Better Cost Estimating," *Communications of the ACM,* February 1992, pp. 51–59. The Standish Group, "Charting the Seas of Information Technology," Dennis, MA: The Standish Group, 1994. Jones, Capers, *Assessment and Control of Software Risks,* Englewood Cliffs, NJ: Yourdon Press, 1994.

12. Jones, Capers, *Assessment and Control of Software Risks,* Englewood Cliffs, NJ: Yourdon Press, 1994.

CHAPTER THREE

Cargo Cult Software Engineering

In the South Seas there is a cargo cult of people. During the war they saw airplanes with lots of good materials, and they want the same thing to happen now. So they've arranged to make things like runways, to put fires along the sides of the runways, to make a wooden hut for a man to sit in, with two wooden pieces on his head for headphones and bars of bamboo sticking out like antennas—he's the controller—and they wait for the airplanes to land. They're doing everything right. The form is perfect. It looks exactly the way it looked before. But it doesn't work. No airplanes land. So I call these things cargo cult science, because they follow all the apparent precepts and forms of scientific investigation, but they're missing something essential, because the planes don't land.

RICHARD FEYNMAN[1]

I find it useful to draw a contrast between two different organizational development styles: "process-oriented" and "commitment-oriented" development. Process-oriented development achieves its effectiveness through skillful planning, use of carefully defined processes, efficient use of available time, and skillful application of software engineering best practices. This style of development succeeds because the organization that uses it is constantly improving. Even if its early attempts are ineffective, steady attention to process means each successive attempt will work better than the previous attempt.

Commitment-oriented development goes by several names including "hero-oriented development" and "individual empowerment." Commitment-oriented organizations are characterized by hiring the best possible people, asking them for total commitment to their projects, empowering them with nearly complete autonomy, motivating them to an extreme degree, and then seeing that they work 60, 80, or 100 hours a week until the project is finished. Commitment-oriented development derives its potency from its tremendous motivational ability—study after study has found that individual motivation is by far the largest single contributor to productivity.[2] Developers make voluntary, personal commitments to the projects they work on, and they often go to extraordinary lengths to make their projects succeed.

Software Imposters

When used knowledgeably, either development style can produce high-quality software economically and quickly. But both development styles have pathological look-alikes that don't work nearly as well, and that can be difficult to distinguish from the genuine articles.

The process-imposter organization bases its practices on a slavish devotion to process for process's sake. These organizations look at process-oriented organizations such as NASA's Software Engineering Laboratory and IBM's former Federal Systems Division. They observe that those organizations generate lots of documents and hold frequent meetings. They conclude that if they generate an equivalent number of documents and hold a comparable number of meetings they will be similarly successful. If they generate more documentation and hold more meetings, they will be even more successful! But they don't understand that the documentation and the meetings are not responsible for the success; they are the side effects of a few specific effective processes. We call these organizations *bureaucratic* because they put the form of software processes above the substance. Their misuse of process is demotivating, which hurts productivity. And they're not very enjoyable to work for.

The commitment-imposter organization focuses primarily on motivating people to work long hours. These organizations look at successful companies like Microsoft, observe that they generate very little documentation, offer stock options to their employees, and then require them to work mountains of overtime. They conclude that if they, too, minimize documentation, offer stock options, and require extensive overtime, they will be successful. The less documentation and the more overtime, the better! But these organizations miss the fact that Microsoft and other successful commitment-oriented companies don't *require* overtime. They hire people who love to create software. They team these people with other people who love to create software just as much as they do. They provide lavish organizational support and rewards for creating software. And then they turn them loose. The natural outcome is that software developers and managers choose to work long hours voluntarily. Imposter organizations confuse the effect (long hours) with the cause (high motivation). We call the imposter organizations *sweatshops* because they emphasize working hard rather than working smart, and they tend to be chaotic and ineffective. They're not very enjoyable to work for either.

Cargo Cult Software Engineering

At first glance, these two kinds of imposter organizations appear to be exact opposites. One is incredibly bureaucratic, and the other is incredibly chaotic. But one key similarity is actually more important than their superficial differences. Neither is very effective, and the reason is that neither understands what really makes its projects succeed or fail. They go through the motions of looking like effective organizations that are stylistically similar. But without any real understanding of why the practices work, they are essentially just sticking pieces of bamboo in their ears and hoping their projects will land safely. Many of their projects end up crashing because these are just two different varieties of cargo cult software engineering, similar in their lack of understanding of what makes software projects work.

Cargo cult software engineering is easy to identify. Cargo cult software engineers justify their practices by saying, "We've always done it this way in the past," or "our company standards require us to do it this way"—even when the specific ways make no sense. They refuse to acknowledge the tradeoffs involved in either process-oriented or commitment-oriented development. Both have strengths and weaknesses. When presented with more effective new practices, cargo cult software engineers prefer to stay in their wooden huts of familiar and comfortable but not-necessarily-effective work habits. "Doing the same thing again and again and expecting different results is a sign of insanity," the old saying goes. It's also a sign of cargo cult software engineering.

The Real Debate

Software pundits often spend time debating whether process is good or individual empowerment (in other words, commitment-oriented development) might be better. This is a false dichotomy. Process *is* good, and so is individual empowerment. The two can exist side by side. Process-oriented organizations can ask for an extreme commitment on specific projects. Commitment-oriented organizations can use software engineering practices skillfully.

The difference between these two approaches really comes down to differences of style and personality. I have worked on several projects of each style, and have liked different things about each style. Some developers enjoy working methodically on an 8 to 5 schedule, which is more common in process-oriented companies. Other developers enjoy the focus and excitement that comes with making a 24×7 commitment to a project. Commitment-oriented projects are more exciting on average, but a process-oriented project can be just as exciting when it has a well-defined and inspiring mission. Process-oriented organizations seem to degenerate into their pathological look-alikes less often than commitment-oriented organizations do, but either style can work well if it is skillfully planned and executed by capable people.

The fact that both process-oriented and commitment-oriented projects have pathological look-alikes has muddied the debate. Some projects conducted in each style succeed, and some fail. That allows a process advocate to point to the process successes and the commitment failures and claim that process is the key to success. It allows the commitment advocate to do the same thing.

The issue that has fallen by the wayside while we've been debating process vs. commitment is so blatant that, like Edgar Allan Poe's purloined letter, it may simply have been so obvious that we have overlooked it. We should not be debating process vs. commitment; we should be debating competence vs. incompetence. The real difference is not which style is chosen, but what education, training, and understanding is brought to bear on the project. Rather than debating process vs. commitment, we should be looking for ways to raise the average level of developer and manager competence. That will improve our chances of success regardless of which development style we choose.

Notes

1. Hutchings, Edward, "*Surely You're Joking, Mr. Feynman!*", New York: W. W. Norton & Company, Reprint Edition, 1997.

2. Boehm, Barry W., *Software Engineering Economics,* Englewood Cliffs, NJ: Prentice-Hall, Inc., 1981.

CHAPTER FOUR

Software Engineering,
Not Computer Science

A scientist builds in order to learn; an engineer learns in order to build.

FRED BROOKS

When interviewing candidates for programming jobs, one of my favorite interview questions is, "How would you describe your approach to software development?" I give them examples such as carpenter, fire fighter, architect, artist, author, explorer, scientist, and archeologist, and I invite them to come up with their own answers. Some candidates try to second-guess what I want to hear; they usually tell me they see themselves as "scientists." Hot-shot coders tell me they see themselves as commandos or swat-team members. My favorite answer came from a candidate who said, "During software design, I'm an architect. When I'm designing the user interface, I'm an artist. During construction, I'm a craftsman. And during unit testing, I'm one mean son of a bitch!"

I like to pose this question because it gets at a fundamental issue in our field: What is the best way to think of software development? Is it science? Is it art? Is it craft? Is it something else entirely?

"Is" vs. "Should"

We have a long tradition in the software field of debating whether software development is art or science. Thirty years ago, Donald Knuth began writing a seven-volume series, *The Art of Computer Programming.* The first three volumes stand at 2,200 pages, suggesting the full seven might amount to more than 5,000 pages. If that's what the *art* of computer programming looks like, I'm not sure I ever want to see the *science*!

People who advocate programming as art point to the aesthetic aspects of software development and argue that science does not allow for such inspiration and creative freedom. People who advocate programming as science point to many programs' high error rates and argue that such low reliability is intolerable—creative freedom be damned. Both these views are incomplete and both ask the wrong question. Software development is art. It is science. It is craft, archeology, fire fighting, sociology, and a host of other activities. It is amateurish in some quarters, professional in others. It is as many different things as there are different people programming. But the proper question is not "What *is* software development currently?" but rather "What *should* professional software development be?" In my opinion, the answer to that question is clear: Professional software development should be engineering. Is it? No. But should it be? Unquestionably, yes.

Engineering vs. Science

With only about 40 percent of software developers holding computer science degrees and practically none holding degrees in software engineering, we shouldn't be surprised to find people confused about the difference between software engineering and computer science. The distinction between science and engineering in software is the same as the distinction in other fields.[1] Scientists learn what is true, how to test hypotheses, and how to extend knowledge in their field. Engineers learn what is true, what is useful, and how to apply well-understood knowledge to solve practical problems. Scientists must keep up to date with the latest research. Engineers must be familiar with knowledge that has already proven to be reliable and effective. If you are doing science, you can afford to be narrow and specialized. If you are doing engineering, you need a broad understanding of all the factors that affect the product you are designing. Scientists don't have to be regulated because they are chiefly accountable to other scientists. Engineers do have to be regulated because they are chiefly accountable to the public. An undergraduate science education prepares students to continue their studies. An undergraduate engineering education prepares students to enter the workforce immediately after completing their studies.

Universities award computer science degrees, and they normally expect their computer science students to obtain software development jobs in which they will immediately begin solving real-world problems. Only a small fraction of computer science undergraduates go on to graduate school or research environments in which they are advancing the state of knowledge about software or computers.

This puts computer science students into a technological no-man's land. They are called scientists, but they are performing job functions that are traditionally performed by engineers, without the benefit of engineering training. The effect is roughly the same as it would be if you assigned a physics Ph.D. to design electrical equipment for commercial sale. The physicist might understand the electrical principles better than the engineers he is working with. But his experience in building equipment is in creating prototypes that are used to advance the state of knowledge in a laboratory. He does not have experience or training in designing rugged, economical equipment that provides practical solutions in real-world settings. We would expect the equipment designed by the physics Ph.D. to work, but perhaps to lack some of the robustness that would make it usable or safe outside a laboratory. Or the equipment might use materials in a way that's acceptable for a single prototype but extravagantly wasteful when units are manufactured by the thousands.

Situations resembling this simple physics example occur literally thousands of times each year in software. When workers educated as computer scientists begin working on production systems, they often design and build software that is too frail for production use, or that's unsafe. They focus narrowly and deeply on minor considerations to the exclusion of other factors that are more important. They might spend two days hand-tuning a sorting algorithm instead of two hours using a code library or copying a suitable algorithm from a book. The typical computer science graduate typically needs several years of on-the-job training to accumulate enough practical knowledge to build minimally satisfactory production software without supervision. Without appropriate formal education, some software developers work their entire careers without acquiring this knowledge.

The lack of professional development isn't solely the software developer's failure. The software world has become a victim of its own success. The software job market has been growing faster than the educational infrastructure needed to support it, and so more than half the people holding software development jobs have been educated in subjects other than software. Employers can't require these software retreads to obtain the equivalent of an undergraduate engineering degree in their off hours. Even if they could, most of the courses available are in computer science, not software engineering. The educational infrastructure has fallen behind industry's needs.

Beyond the Buzzword

Some people think that "software engineering" is just a buzzword that means the same thing as "computer programming." Admittedly, "software engineering" has been misused. But a term can be abused and still have a legitimate meaning.

The dictionary definition of "engineering" is the application of scientific and mathematical principles toward practical ends. That is what most programmers try to do. We apply scientifically developed and mathematically defined algorithms, functional design methods, quality-assurance methods, and other practices to develop software products and services. As David Parnas points out, in other technical fields the engineering professions were invented and given legal standing so that customers could know who was qualified to build technical products.[2] Software customers deserve no less.

Some people think that treating software development as engineering means we'll all have to use formal methods—writing programs as mathematical proofs. Common sense and experience tell us that that is overkill for many projects. Others object that commercial software is too dependent on changing market conditions to permit careful, time-consuming engineering.

These objections are based upon a narrow and mistaken idea of engineering. Engineering is the application of scientific principles toward *practical* ends. If the engineering isn't practical, it's bad engineering. Trying to apply formal methods to all software projects is as bad an idea as trying to apply code-and-fix development to all projects.

Treating software as engineering makes clearer the idea that different development goals are appropriate for different projects. When a building is designed, the construction materials must suit the building's purpose. I can build a large equipment shed to store farming vehicles from thin, uninsulated sheet metal. I wouldn't build a house the same way. But even though the house is sturdier and warmer, we wouldn't refer to the shed as being inferior to the house in any way. The shed has been designed appropriately for its intended purpose. If it had been built the same way as a house, we might even criticize it for being "over-engineered"—a judgment that the designers wasted resources in building it and that it actually isn't well engineered.

In software, a well-run project can be managed to meet any of the following product objectives:

- Minimal defects
- Maximum user satisfaction
- Minimal response time
- Good maintainability
- Good extendibility
- High robustness
- High correctness

Each software project team should define the relative importance of each characteristic explicitly, and then the project team should conduct the project in a way that achieves its objectives.

Software projects are different from engineering projects that use physical materials. In other kinds of engineering, the cost of materials can contribute 50 percent or more of the total project cost. Some engineering companies report that they automatically regard projects with labor constituting more than 50 percent of project cost as high risk.[3] On a typical software project, labor costs can contribute almost 100 percent of the total project cost. Most engineering projects focus on optimizing *product* goals; design costs are relatively insignificant. Because labor cost makes up such a large part of total lifetime software costs, software projects need to focus more on optimizing *project* goals than other kinds of engineering do. So, in addition to working toward product objectives, a software team might also work to achieve any of the following project objectives:

- Short schedule
- Predictable delivery date
- Low cost
- Small team size
- Flexibility to make mid-project feature-set changes

Each software project must strike a balance among various project and product goals. We don't want to pay $5,000 for a word processor, nor do we want one that crashes every 15 minutes.

Which of these specific product and project characteristics a project team emphasizes does not determine whether a project is a true "software engineering" project. Some projects need to produce software with minimal defects and near-perfect correctness—software for medical equipment, avionics, anti-lock brakes, and so on. Most people would agree that these projects are an appropriate domain for full-blown software engineering. Other projects need to deliver their software with adequate reliability but with low costs and short schedules. Are these properly the domain of software engineering? One informal definition of engineering is "doing for a dime what anyone can do for a dollar." Lots of software projects today are doing for a dollar what any good software engineer could do for a dime. Economical development is also the domain of software engineering.

Today's pervasive reliance on code-and-fix development—and the cost and schedule overruns that go with it—is not the result of a software engineering calculation, but of too little education and training in software engineering practices.

The Right Questions

Software development as it's commonly practiced today doesn't look much like engineering, but it could. Once we stop asking the wrong question—"What *is* software development currently?"—and start asking the right question—"*Should* professional software development be engineering?"—we can start answering the really interesting questions. What is software engineering's core body of knowledge? What needs to be done before professional software developers can use that knowledge? How big is the payback from practicing software development as an engineering discipline? What are appropriate standards of professional conduct for software developers? For software organizations? Should software developers be regulated? If so, to what extent? And, perhaps the most interesting question of all: What will the software industry look like after all these questions have been answered?

Notes

1. For much of this discussion, I am indebted to David L. Parnas, especially for his paper, "Software Engineering Programmes Are Not Computer Science Programmes," *IEEE Software,* November/December 1999.

2. Parnas, David L., "Software Engineering: An Unconsummated Marriage," *Software Engineering Notes,* November 1997.

3. Baines, Robin, "Across Disciplines: Risk, Design, Method, Process, and Tools," *IEEE Software,* July/August 1998, pp. 61–64.

CHAPTER FIVE

Body of Knowledge

Truth will sooner come out of error than from confusion.

FRANCIS BACON

A person needs to know about 50,000 chunks of information to be an expert in a field, where a chunk is any piece of knowledge that can be remembered rather than derived.[1] In mature fields, it typically takes at least ten years for a world-class expert to acquire that much knowledge. Some people have argued that software-related knowledge isn't stable enough to be codified into a well-defined body of knowledge. They say that half of what a person needs to know to develop software today will be obsolete within three years. If the half-life claim is true, in the 10 years it would take an expert to learn 50,000 chunks of information, 30,000 of those chunks would become obsolete. Would-be software engineers would be like Sisyphus, pushing a boulder up a mountain only to have the boulder roll down the mountain as soon as it reaches the top.

What are the half-lives of Java, Perl, C++, Linux, and Microsoft Windows? All these technologies are highly relevant as I write this, but will they still be relevant by the time you read this? The half-life claim might well be true for technology-related knowledge. But there is another kind of software development knowledge that is likely to serve a professional programmer throughout his or her career, and that knowledge is not subject to these same limitations.

Essence and Accident

In 1987, Fred Brooks published an influential article, "No Silver Bullets—Essence and Accidents of Software Engineering."[2] Its main contention is that no single tool or methodology—no "silver bullet"—portended a 10 to 1 improvement in productivity over the next decade. The reasoning behind this claim helps in identifying software development knowledge not subject to the three-year half-life.

In using the words "essence" and "accident," Brooks draws on an ancient philosophical tradition of distinguishing between "essential" and "accidental" properties. Essential properties are those properties that a thing must have to be that thing: A car must have an engine, wheels, and a transmission to be a car. These are essential properties. A car might have a V8 or an in-line six, studded snow tires or racing slicks, an automatic transmission or a stick shift. These are "accidental" properties, the properties that arise by happenstance and do not affect the basic "car-ness" of the car. The term "accidental" can be confusing, but it just means nonessential or optional.

According to Brooks, the most difficult work of software development is not that of representing the concepts faithfully in a specific computer programming language (coding) or checking the fidelity of that representation (testing). That is the accidental part of software development. The essence of software development, Brooks argues, consists of working out the specification, design, and verification of a highly precise and richly detailed set of interlocking concepts. He says that software is difficult because of its essential complexity, conformity, changeability, and invisibility.

Computer programs are *complex* by nature. Even if you could invent a programming language that operated exactly at the level of the problem domain, programming would still be a complicated activity because you would still need to precisely define relationships between real-world entities, identify exception cases, anticipate all possible state transitions, and so on. Strip away the accidental work involved in representing these factors in a specific programming language and in a specific computing environment, and you will still have the essential difficulty of defining the underlying real-world concepts and debugging your understanding of them.

Another essential difficulty arises from the need for software to *conform* to messy real-world constraints such as pre-existing hardware, third-party components, government regulations, business rules, and legacy data formats. The software designer often faces inflexible external considerations that limit the extent to which complexity can be reduced.

Software's *changeability* presents another essential difficulty. The more successful a program is, the more uses people will find for it, and the more it will be adapted beyond the domain for which it was originally intended. As the software grows, it will become more complex and will need to conform to additional constraints. The more software is adapted, the more involved the adaptations become.

A final source of essential difficulty arises from software's inherent *invisibility.* Software can't be visualized with 2-D or 3-D geometric models. Attempts to visually represent even simple logic flow quickly become absurdly complicated, as anyone who has ever tried to draw a flow chart for even a simple program will attest.

Brooks argues that software development has already made all possible major gains in the accidental elements. These gains include the invention of high-level languages, adoption of interactive computing, and development of powerful integrated environments. Any further order-of-magnitude productivity improvements, he says, can be made only by addressing software's essential difficulties: the complexity, conformity, changeability, and invisibility inherent in software development.

Defining a Stable Core

Knowledge that helps developers deal with what Brooks calls the "essential difficulties" of software development is what I think of as "software engineering principles," which make up software engineering's core body of knowledge. In 1968, NATO held the first conference on software engineering. Using the term "software engineering" to describe the body of knowledge that existed at that time was premature, and it was intended to be provocative.

Exactly how small was the stable core in 1968? Consider that the first fully correct binary search algorithm was published in 1962, only six years before the NATO conference.[3] C. Böhm and G. Jacopini published the paper that established the theoretical foundation for eliminating the *goto* and the creation of structured programming only two years before the conference.[4] Edsger Dijkstra wrote his famous letter to the editor, "GoTo Statement Considered Harmful," in 1968.[5] At the time the conference was held, subroutines were a fairly new idea, and programmers regularly debated whether they were really useful. Larry Constantine, Glenford Myers, and Wayne Stevens didn't publish the first paper on structured design until six years after the conference in 1974.[6] Tom Gilb published the first book on software metrics in 1977,[7] and Tom DeMarco published the first book on software requirements analysis in 1979.[8] Anyone who tried to identify a stable core of knowledge in 1968 would have had their work cut out for them.

From an analysis of the SWEBOK project's Body of Knowledge areas (which I'll discuss later in this chapter), I estimate that the half-life of software engineering's body of knowledge in 1968 was only about 10 years. As Figure 5-1 illustrates, the stable core was relatively small, and I estimate that only about 10 to 20 percent of software engineering knowledge from 1968 is still in use today.

Software engineering has made significant progress since 1968. Hundreds of thousands of pages have been written about software engineering. Professional societies host hundreds of conferences and workshops every year. Knowledge has been codified into more than 2,000 pages of IEEE software engineering standards. Dozens of universities across North America offer graduate education in software engineering, and dozens more have recently begun to offer undergraduate programs.

The fact that we do not have perfectly stable knowledge of software engineering practices hardly makes software engineering unique. In the 1930s, the medical profession did not yet know about penicillin, the structure of DNA, or the genetic basis of many diseases, and it did not have technologies such as heart-lung machines and magnetic resonance imaging. And yet there was a profession of medicine.

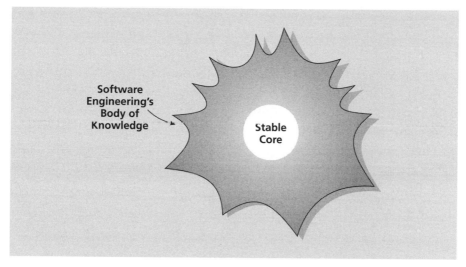

FIGURE 5-1

As of the 1968 NATO Conference on Software Engineering, only about 10 to 20 percent of the software engineering body of knowledge was stable (i.e., would still be relevant 30 years later). The half-life of the software engineering body of knowledge at that time was about 10 years.

As Figure 5-2 suggests, based on my SWEBOK knowledge-area analysis, I estimate that as of 2003 the stable core now makes up about 50 percent of the knowledge needed to develop a software system. That might not seem like a dramatic change from the 10 to 20 percent of 1968, but it implies that the body of knowledge's half-life has improved from about 10 years to about 30 years. That means that the educational investment a person makes at the beginning of a career in software will remain largely relevant throughout that person's career.

Stabilization of software engineering's body of knowledge puts software engineering on an educational footing similar to other engineering disciplines. As David Parnas points out, the content of a physics class can remain unchanged even if the lab gets a new oscilloscope. Most of the content of software engineering courses can be independent of specific, relatively short-lived technologies like C++ and Java. Students will have to

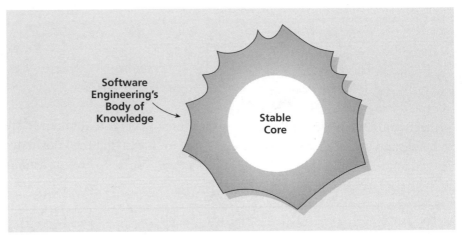

FIGURE 5-2

As of 2003, about 50 percent of the software engineering body of knowledge is stable and will still be relevant 30 years from now.

learn those technologies in the lab, but in the classroom they can focus on more lasting knowledge.

Software Engineering's Body of Knowledge

In Chapter 4, I argued that software engineering is not the same as computer science, but if it isn't computer science, what is it? Those of us working in software development now have an exciting opportunity to see a new field being born. For more established fields like mathematics, physics, and psychology, we tend to take the contents of the field for granted, assuming that the definition of what is in and what is out of the field has always been the way it is and has to be that way. But at some point people working in each field developed textbooks and university curriculums that required them to decide what knowledge was in and what was out. For hundreds of years, people didn't differentiate between mathematics, physics, psychology, and philosophy. Mathematics began to be treated as separate from philosophy about 300 A.D.. Physics began to be treated as separate from philosophy about 1600. Psychology wasn't distinguished from philosophy until about 1900.

In defining what knowledge is in and what is out of the field of software engineering, experts have recommended that the focus should be on generally accepted knowledge and practices. As Figure 5-3 suggests, "generally accepted" refers to the knowledge and practices that are applicable to most projects most of the time—practices that most experts would agree are valuable and useful. Generally accepted does not mean that the knowledge and practices should be applied uniformly to all projects. Project leaders will still be responsible for determining the most appropriate practices for any particular project.[9]

Since 1968, we've made significant progress in the areas Brooks referred to as the "essential difficulties" of software development. We now have adequate or good reference books on requirements engineering, design,

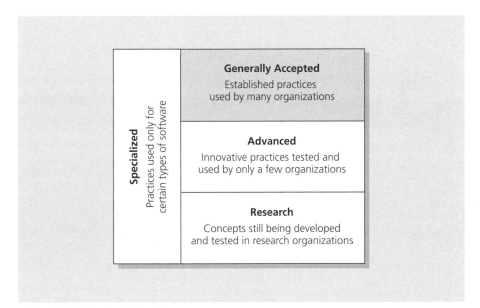

FIGURE 5-3

Categories of possible knowledge in the software engineering body of knowledge. The focus of defining the knowledge needed by a professional software engineer is on generally accepted knowledge.

Source: Adapted from "Professionalism of Software Engineering: Next Steps"[10]

construction, testing, reviews, quality assurance, software project management, algorithms, and user interface design, just to name a few topics. New and better books that codify software engineering knowledge are appearing regularly. Some core elements have not yet been brought together in practical textbooks or courses, and in that sense our body of knowledge is still under construction. But the basic knowledge about how to perform each of these practices is available—in journal articles, conference papers, and seminars as well as books. (These books are listed on the software engineering professional Web site described at the back of the book.) The pioneers of software engineering have already blazed the trails and surveyed the land. Now the software engineering settlers need to build the roads and develop the rest of the education and accreditation infrastructure.

Researchers at the Université du Québec à Montréal have spearheaded an effort to identify the generally accepted elements of software engineering. This effort has been coordinated by the ACM and the IEEE Computer Society and involves both academic and industrial participants. This effort is called the Software Engineering Body of Knowledge project, or SWEBOK.[11]

As Figure 5-4 suggests, software engineering draws from computer science, mathematics, cognitive sciences (psychology and sociology), project management, and various engineering disciplines.

From this starting point, SWEBOK has identified knowledge areas that make up the core competencies for a professional software engineer.[12]

- *Software Requirements.* The discovery, documentation, and analysis of the functions to be implemented in software.
- *Software Design.* Definition of the basic structure of the system at the architectural and detailed levels, division into modules, definition of interfaces for modules, and choice of algorithms within modules.
- *Software Construction.* Implementation of the software including detailed design, coding, debugging, unit testing, technical reviews, and performance optimization. This area overlaps somewhat with Software Design and Software Testing.

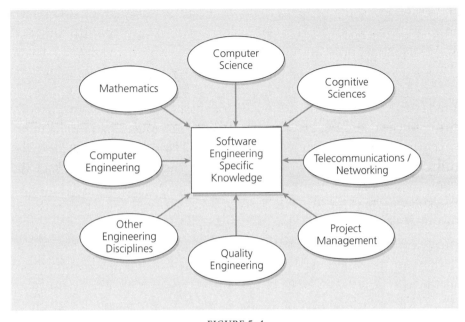

FIGURE 5-4

Sources of knowledge in software engineering's body of knowledge.

Source: Adapted from "Professionalism of Software Engineering: Next Steps"[13]

- *Software Testing.* All activities associated with executing software to detect defects and evaluate features. Testing includes test planning, test case design, and specific kinds of tests including development tests, unit tests, component tests, integration tests, system tests, regression tests, stress tests, and acceptance tests.

- *Software Maintenance.* Revision and enhancement of existing software, related documentation, and tests.

- *Software Configuration Management.* Identification, documentation, and change control of all intellectual property generated on a software project including source code, content (graphics, sound, text, and video), requirements, designs, test materials, estimates, plans, and user documentation.

- *Software Quality.* All activities associated with providing confidence that a software item conforms or will conform to technical requirements. Quality engineering includes quality assurance planning, quality measurement, reliability, testing, technical reviews, audits, and verification and validation.

- *Software Engineering Management.* Planning, tracking, and controlling of a software project, software work, or a software organization.

- *Software Engineering Tools and Methods.* Tool and methodology support, such as CASE tools, reusable code libraries, and formal methods, including practices for adopting and disseminating tools and methods within an organization.

- *Software Engineering Process.* Activities related to improving software development quality, timeliness, productivity, and other project and product characteristics.

The extent of this list might surprise some people. Many practicing programmers work as though software construction is the only knowledge area that matters. As important as that area is, it is only one of ten areas that a professional software engineer should know.

Other practicing programmers might be surprised at the complete absence of specific languages and programming environments—Java, C++, Visual Basic, Linux, and so on. That's because the body of knowledge emphasizes software engineering principles rather than technology knowledge.

A few people's reaction to these knowledge areas will be, "That's a lot to expect someone to learn just to write computer programs." It is a lot to expect someone to learn, and historically we've been expecting them to learn it implicitly, through on-the-job exposure to new information. The result is that most practicing computer programmers have pretty good knowledge of Software Construction and Software Maintenance; marginal knowledge of Software Requirements, Software Design, Software Testing, and Software Engineering Tools and Methods; and virtually no knowledge of Software Configuration Management, Software Quality, Software Engineering Management, or Software Engineering Process.

I don't expect software engineers to achieve mastery in each of these areas, but a professional software engineer should at least acquire introductory knowledge of all areas, competence in most, and mastery of some.

As I described in Chapter 4, one of the differences between a scientist and an engineer is that scientists can afford to have knowledge that is narrow and deep, but engineers need a broad understanding of all the factors that affect the products they create.

Planting a Stake

Is this definition of software engineering's body of knowledge the final answer? No. The field of medicine has continued to evolve, and the field of software engineering will continue to evolve too. But there is great value in planting a stake in the ground and saying, "This is what constitutes the software engineering body of knowledge at this time."

As Francis Bacon pointed out when he laid the foundation for modern science 350 years ago, errors are a better basis for progress than confusion is. Bacon knew that when his approach was used many of the initial conclusions—the "first vintages"—would be mistaken, but that was part of his plan. Major elements of our current definition of the software engineering body of knowledge will undoubtedly turn out to be mistaken, but an imperfect, clear definition will give us a baseline upon which we can improve. Exchanging the current confused muddle for a clearly defined body of knowledge is a good trade, errors and all.

Notes

1. Shaw, Mary, "Prospects for an Engineering Discipline of Software," *IEEE Software,* November 1990, pp. 15ff.

2. Brooks, Frederick P., Jr., "No Silver Bullets—Essence and Accidents of Software Engineering," *Computer,* April 1987, pp. 10–19.

3. Knuth, Donald, *The Art of Computer Programming, Volume 3: Sorting and Searching,* Reading, MA: Addison-Wesley, 1973, p. 419.

4. "Flow Diagrams, Turing Machines, and Languages with Only Two Formation Rules," *Communications of the ACM,* May 1966, pp. 366–371.

5. *Communications of the ACM,* Vol. 11, 1968, pp. 148ff. Also available from www.cs.utexas.edu/users/EWD/ewd02xx/EWD215.PDF.

6. "Structured Design," *IBM Systems Journal,* No. 2, 1974, pp. 115–139.

7. *Software Metrics,* Cambridge, MA: Winthrop Publishers, 1977.

8. *Structured Analysis and System Specification,* NJ: Prentice Hall, 1979.

9. Duncan, W. R., "A Guide to the Project Management Body of Knowledge," Upper Darby, PA: Project Management Institute, 1996.

10. Tripp, Leonard, "Professionalism of Software Engineering: Next Steps," Keynote Address at *12th Conference on Software Engineering Education and Training,* March 22, 1999.

11. Additional information is available on the SWEBOK Web site at www.swebok.org.

12. "Guide to the Software Engineering Body of Knowledge: Trial Version (Version 1.00)," Alain Abran, et al., IEEE Computer Society, 2001.

13. Tripp, Leonard, "Professionalism of Software Engineering: Next Steps," Keynote Address at *12th Conference on Software Engineering Education and Training,* March 22, 1999.

CHAPTER SIX

Novum Organum

A prudent question is one-half of wisdom.

FRANCIS BACON

In 1620, Francis Bacon published the *Novum Organum,* a masterwork that challenged Bacon's contemporaries to discard their ancient reliance on pure deductive reasoning and embrace a scientific method based on observation and experience. He imagined a new world of culture and leisure that could be gained by inquiry into the laws and processes of nature. In describing this world, he anticipated the effects of advances in science, engineering, and technology.

Bacon's scientific method consisted of three steps:

1. Purge your mind of prejudices—what Bacon called "superstition."
2. Collect observations and experiences systematically.
3. Stop, survey what you have seen, and draw initial conclusions (the "first vintage").

Novum Organum was part of a larger work called *Instauratio Magna,* which set out to organize the sciences, define a method of scientific inquiry, collect observations and facts, present examples of the new method, and define a new philosophy based on the results of this scientific work. This work so influenced modern scientific methods that Bacon is often called the Father of Modern Science.

The title page of *Instauratio Magna* contained an image of a ship passing through the Pillars of Hercules (Figure 6-1). The Pillars of Hercules were generally accepted to have stood on the sides of the Strait of Gibraltar,

FIGURE 6-1

This is the title page from Bacon's Instauratio Magna, *which contains his* Novum Organum. *The ancients were reluctant to sail beyond the Pillars of Hercules.*

the sole passage between the Mediterranean Sea and the Atlantic Ocean. For the ancients, the Pillars of Hercules symbolized the limits of possible human exploration. Beyond the pillars lay the edge of the earth; the ancients had not been inclined to progress into those outer reaches and leave the old world behind.

At this time, average software development practices are becalmed in a windless sea of code-and-fix programming—a kind of flat earth approach to software development that was proved ineffective 20 years ago. Leading software engineers have a clear idea of what lies beyond software's Pillars of Hercules—software engineering has already had its Marco Polo, Vasco da Gama, and Ferdinand Magellan who have explored the new world of better software engineering practices. As Chapter 12 will describe, vast software riches await in waters that have been charted extensively but are traveled infrequently by average software practitioners.

Profession Defined

Considering the disparity between the best software organizations and the worst, the current challenge is not so much to advance the state of the art as it is to raise the average level of practice. The new world has been adequately explored; it's time to start colonizing. The traditional means of raising the level of practice in a field, especially one that affects the public welfare, is through establishment of a formal profession.

Although the term is often used casually, the notion of a "profession" has a long and well-defined legal standing. The Code of Federal Regulations (CFR) in the United States says that a person employed in a "professional capacity" can be distinguished by several characteristics.

A professional's work typically requires advanced knowledge in science or a field of learning that is acquired through a prolonged course of specialized study. The CFR distinguishes this from a general academic education. It also distinguishes it from training in routine processes, whether they be mental, manual, or physical. The CFR goes on to note that professional work can be creative and artistic. The work may depend primarily on the inventiveness, imagination, or talent of the person doing the work.

The CFR states that professional work requires the consistent exercise of discretion and judgment in its performance. The work is predominantly intellectual and varied in character. The CFR again differentiates this from routine mental, manual, or physical work.

Most software developers will recognize characteristics of their own work in the CFR's description of a profession. The work certainly requires advanced knowledge (detailed technical knowledge, anyway), and it benefits from specialized instruction and study. Software development contains a significant creative element, and clearly calls for a great deal of discretion and judgment. In short, the work performed by software developers seems clearly to meet the definition of "professional work" as defined in the CFR.

The CFR contributes part of the legal definition of a profession. The body of legal precedents (court cases) establish a slightly different but complementary definition. According to legal precedents, a profession has:[1]

- A requirement for extensive learning and training
- A code of ethics imposing standards higher than those normally tolerated in the marketplace
- A disciplinary system for professionals who breach the code
- A primary emphasis on social responsibility over strictly individual gain, and a corresponding duty of its members to behave as members of a disciplined and honorable profession
- A prerequisite of a license prior to admission to practice

How well does software rate according to these criteria?

In Search of a Software Engineering Profession

Gary Ford and Norman E. Gibbs of the Software Engineering Institute identified eight elements of a mature profession.[2] A professional's development typically follows the progression shown in Figure 6-2.

Initial Professional Education. Professionals generally begin their professional life by completing a university program in their chosen field—medical school, engineering school, law school, and so on.

Accreditation. University programs are accredited by oversight bodies that determine whether each program provides adequate education. This ensures that, as long as professionals graduate from accredited programs, they will start their professional lives with the knowledge they need to perform effectively. The Accreditation Board for Engineering and Technology (ABET) oversees engineering programs in the United States, and the Canadian Engineering Accreditation Board (CEAB) oversees engineering programs in Canada.

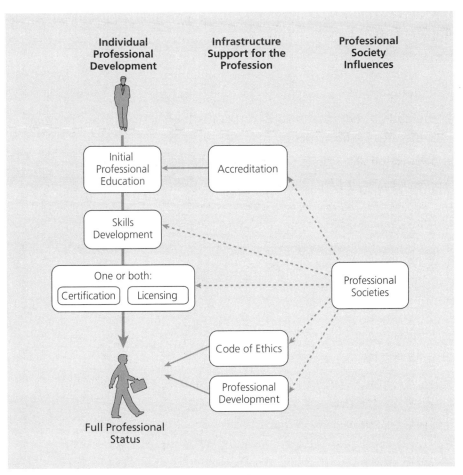

FIGURE 6-2

Professional development follows most or all of these basic steps in all well-established professions.

Skills Development. For most professions, education alone is not sufficient to develop full professional capabilities. Nascent professionals need practice applying their knowledge before they are prepared to take primary responsibility for performing work in their field. Physicians have a three-year residency. Certified Public Accountants (CPAs) must work one year for a board-approved organization before receiving their licenses. Professional Engineers must have at least four years of work experience. Requiring some kind of apprenticeship ensures that people who enter a profession have practice performing work at a satisfactory level of competence.

Certification. After completion of education and skills development, a professional is required to pass one or more exams that ensure the person has attained a minimum level of knowledge. Doctors take board exams. Accountants take CPA exams. Professional engineers take a Fundamentals of Engineering exam at college graduation time and then take an engineering specialty exam about four years later. Some professions require recertification from time to time.

Licensing. Licensing is similar to certification except that it is mandatory instead of voluntary and administered by a governmental authority.

Professional Development. Many professionals are required to keep their professional education current. Ongoing professional education maintains or improves workers' knowledge and skills after they begin professional practice. Professional development requirements tend to be strongest in professions where there is a rapidly changing body of technical knowledge. Medicine is perhaps the most notable because of the constant improvements in drugs, therapies, medical equipment, and diagnosis and treatment procedures. After a professional's initial education and skills development are complete, this requirement helps to ensure a minimum competency level throughout the professional's career.

Professional Societies. Professionals see themselves as part of a community of like-minded individuals who put their professional standards above their individual self-interest or their employer's self-interest. In the beginning, professional societies usually promote the exchange of knowledge, and over time their function evolves to include defining certification criteria, managing certification programs, establishing accreditation standards, and defining codes of ethics and disciplinary action for violations of those codes.

Code of Ethics. Each profession has a code of ethics to ensure that its practitioners behave responsibly. The code states not just what its practitioners actually do, but what they should do. Professionals can be ejected from their professional societies or lose their license to practice for violating the code of ethics. Adherence to a recognized code of conduct helps professionals feel they belong to a well-regarded community, and enforcement of ethics standards helps maintain a minimum level of conduct.

In addition to the eight elements identified by Ford and Gibbs, many professions exhibit a ninth characteristic that applies to organizations rather than specific workers:

Organizational Certification. In many professions, not only must individuals be certified, their organizations must be certified. Accounting firms are peer reviewed. Hospitals are accredited, as are universities. For fields as complex as accounting, education, and medicine, organizational certification is a response to the reality that individual competence is not sufficient to guarantee adequate levels of professional service; organizational characteristics can have as much influence as individuals' characteristics.

Ford and Gibbs point out that many nonprofessional occupations exhibit some small number of these elements. For example, the state of California requires licenses for custom upholsterers, amateur boxers, private investigators, and mule racing jockeys, but it doesn't require most of the other elements of a profession for those occupations. For all common professions, nearly all of the elements exist.

Ford and Gibbs defined several levels of maturity for each of the elements of a profession.

Nonexistence. The element simply doesn't exist.

Ad Hoc. The element exists, but only in isolated, uncoordinated instances.

Established. The element exists and is clearly identified with a specific profession. (Ford and Gibbs use the word "specific," but I find that confusing.)

Maturing. The element has existed for many years and is actively maintained and improved by some professional body.

A mature profession is one whose elements have reached the maturing stage. Of course, "maturity" is a moving target. Some of the specific elements that seemed mature 30 years ago don't seem mature today, and some elements that seem mature today will not seem mature 30 years from now.

Table 6-1 describes the maturity of the software engineering profession. The profession is mostly in the Established stage, with some areas lagging and some moving into Maturity. More details about the entries in the table are discussed throughout this book.

TABLE 6-1

Maturity of the elements of the software engineering profession[3]

ELEMENT	CURRENT STATUS
Initial Professional Education	Between Ad Hoc and Established. Bachelor's degrees in computer science, electrical engineering, mathematics, and so on are the common preparation for entry into the profession. Dozens of master's degree programs in software engineering exist. Numerous undergraduate programs have been launched in the past few years, but few students have completed those programs so far.
Accreditation	Established. Accreditation guidelines are currently being defined by a working group from the IEEE Computer Society and the ACM but have not yet been implemented.[4]
Skills Development	Established. Guidelines have been developed for the skills needed by a software engineer to enter the profession.
Certification	Established. Commercial vendors such as Microsoft, Novell, and Oracle have provided technology-related certification programs for many years. Since 2002, the IEEE Computer Society has offered a Certified Software Development Professional Certificate for general software engineering credentials.
Licensing	Ad Hoc. The state of Texas licenses professional software engineers under a statute passed in 1998. The provinces of British Columbia and Ontario began registering professional software engineers in 1999.
Professional Development	Ad Hoc, moving toward Established. Some organizations have published professional development guidelines. For examples, see the IEEE Computer Society's continuing education guidelines at www.computer.org/certification and Construx Software's guidelines at www.construx.com/ladder.

TABLE 6-1 *continued*

ELEMENT	CURRENT STATUS
Professional Societies	Established, moving toward Maturing. The IEEE Computer Society, the ACM, and other professional societies exist. These societies (especially the IEEE) explicitly state that they represent software engineering. They do not yet offer the full range of products and services needed to support software engineers as professionals. They cannot discipline violators of the software engineering code of ethics.
Code of Ethics	Established. The ACM and the IEEE Computer Society have adopted a code of ethics specifically for software engineers. The code is not yet widely respected or adopted within industry.
Organizational Certification	Established, moving toward Maturing. The Software Engineering Institute has defined a Software Capability Maturity Model, which it actively maintains and improves. The model has been used to assess more than 1,500 organizations since 1987. It is not applied universally. ISO 9000-9004 certification is widely adopted, especially in Europe.

Through the Pillars

Software engineering does not fully meet the definition of a profession at this time. Widely available initial education is just beginning to emerge. Certification became available only in 2002. Licensing is available to only a tiny fraction of current software workers. A code of ethics exists, but it isn't enforced. Much work is being done, however, to accelerate the movement of software engineering into the Established and Maturing stages.

If we apply Bacon's scientific method to software engineering, we can see the three steps we need to help software engineering reach maturity.

Purge your mind of prejudices. The software industry needs to kick its addiction to code-and-fix development, a prejudice that has a long track record of benefiting no one.

Collect observations and experiences systematically. A few organizations have begun collecting data on the effectiveness of their development practices and evaluating which practices make them most successful. Some have achieved dramatic results. Other organizations need to follow.

Stop, survey what you have seen, and draw initial conclusions. This book presents some initial conclusions.

Software development is at a major decision point. We can stay safe in our code-and-fix harbor, not venturing past the Pillars of Hercules and not achieving the significant gains that have already been discovered by software engineering explorers. Or we can boldly venture toward a new profession of software engineering and begin colonizing a new world of higher productivity, lower costs, shorter schedules, and better quality.

Notes

1. Adapted from Cem Kaner, "Computer Malpractice," *Software QA,* Volume 3, no. 4, 1997, p. 23.

2. From Gary Ford and Norman E. Gibbs, "A Mature Profession of Software Engineering," SEI, CMU, CMU/SEI-96-TR-004, January 1996.

3. Adapted from Gary Ford and Norman E. Gibbs, "A Mature Profession of Software Engineering," SEI, CMU, CMU/SEI-96-TR-004, January 1996.

4. For current status, see sites.computer.org/ccse and www.computer.org/education/cc2001.

PART TWO

Individual Professionalism

CHAPTER SEVEN

Orphans Preferred

*Wanted: Young, skinny, wirey fellows not over 18. Must be
expert riders willing to risk death daily. Orphans preferred.
Wages $25 per week.*

PONY EXPRESS ADVERTISEMENT, 1860

*We realize the skills, intellect and personality we seek are
rare, and our compensation plan reflects that. In return,
we expect TOTAL AND ABSOLUTE COMMITMENT to project
success—overcoming all obstacles to create applications
on time and within budget.*

SOFTWARE DEVELOPER ADVERTISEMENT, 1995[1]

The stereotypical programmer is a shy young man who works in a darkened room, intensely concentrating on magical incantations that make the computer do his bidding. He can concentrate for 12 to 16 hours at a time, often working through the night to make his artistic vision a reality. He subsists on pizza and Twinkies. When interrupted, the programming creature responds violently, hurling strings of cryptic acronyms at his interrupter—"TCP/IP, RPC, RCS, ACM, and IEEE!" he yells. The programmer breaks his intense concentration only to attend Star Trek conventions and watch Monty Python reruns. He is sometimes regarded as an indispensable genius, sometimes as an eccentric artist. Vital information is stored in his head and his head alone. He is secure in his job, knowing that, valuable as he is, precious few people compete for his job.

USA Today reported that the techie nerd stereotype is so well-entrenched that students in every grade ranked computer jobs near the bottom of their lists of career choices.[2] *The Wall Street Journal* reported that film crews have difficulty presenting stories about leading-edge software companies in an interesting way because every story starts with "an office park, a cubicle, and a guy sitting there with a box on his desk."[3] Sometimes the stereotype is fostered even inside the profession. The associate director of Stanford University's computer science program was quoted by *The New York Times* as saying that software jobs are "mind-numbingly boring."[4] This is all in spite of the fact that sources such as the *Jobs Rated Almanac* consistently rate software jobs at the top or near the top of the most desirable occupations.[5]

How much of the stereotype is true, and what effect does it have on the programming occupation? Let's look first at the programmer's personality, then at the other elements of the stereotype.

The Meyers-Briggs Type Indicator

A common means of categorizing personality was developed by Katherine Briggs and Isabel Briggs Meyers and is called the Meyers-Briggs Type Indicator, or MBTI. The MBTI categorizes personality types in four ways.

Extroversion (E) or Introversion (I). Extroverts are oriented toward the outside world of people and things. Introverts are more interested in the inner world of ideas.

Sensing (S) or Intuition (N). This category refers to how a person prefers to receive decision-making data. The sensing person focuses on known facts, concrete data, and experience. The intuitive person looks for possibilities and focuses on concepts and theories.

Thinking (T) or Feeling (F). This mode refers to a person's decision-making style. The thinker makes decisions based on objective analysis and logic; the feeler relies on subjective feelings and emotions.

Perceiving (P) or Judging (J). The perceiving person prefers flexibility and open-ended possibility, whereas the judging person prefers order and control.

To determine MBTI type, a person takes a test that assigns one letter from each of the four categories, resulting in a designation such as ISTJ or ENTJ. These letters indicate an individual's personality tendencies or preferences. They don't necessarily indicate how a person will react in specific circumstances. A person might naturally prefer to be an I, but might have developed her E to be more comfortable in a business setting, for example. Such a person might test as an I even though most business associates would classify her as an extrovert.

MBTI Results for Software Developers

Two large studies have found the most common personality type for software developers is ISTJ,[6] a personality type that tends to be serious and quiet, practical, orderly, logical, and successful through concentration and thoroughness. ISTJs comprise from 25 to 40 percent of software developers.[7]

Consistent with the stereotype, programmers are indeed introverts. One-half to two-thirds of the software development population is introverted compared to about one-quarter of the general population.[8] Part of the reason for the majority of software developers being *I*s might be that more *I*s pursue higher education, and programmers are more educated than average. About 60 percent of software developers have attained at least a bachelor's degree, compared to about 30 percent of the general population.[9]

The S/N (sensing/intuition) and T/F (thinking/feeling) attributes are particularly interesting because they describe an individual's decision-making style. Eighty to 90 percent of software developers are *T*s compared to about 50 percent of the general population.[10] Compared to the average, *T*s are more logical, analytical, scientific, dispassionate, cold, impersonal, concerned with matters of truth, and unconcerned with people's feelings.

Programmers are approximately evenly split between *S*s and *N*s, and the difference between the two will be immediately recognizable to most software developers. *S*s are methodical, live in the world of what can be accomplished now, are precise, concrete, and practical, like to specialize, and like to develop a single idea in depth rather than several ideas at once. *N*s are inventive, live in the world of possibility and theories, like to generalize, and like to explore many alternative ideas. An example of an *S* is an expert programmer who is intimately acquainted with every detail of a specific programming language or technology. An example of an *N* is a designer who considers wide-ranging possibilities and shrugs off low-level technical issues as "implementation details." *S*s sometimes aggravate *N*s because they go deep into technical details before *N*s feel the breadth has been adequately explored. *N*s sometimes aggravate *S*s because they jump from one design idea to the next before *S*s feel they have explored any particular technical area in sufficient depth.

Personality Characteristics of Great Designers

The MBTI gives some insight into typical programmer personalities, but it isn't the final word. One important group of software development skills is software design skills. Many programmers aspire to be great designers. What are the characteristics of great designers? One study[11] of great designers in general (not just software developers) found that the most creative human problem solvers seem to move easily between the S/N, T/F, and P/J ends of the continuum. They move back and forth between holistic and sequential, intuition and logic, theory and specific details. They are able to look at problems from many different points of view. Leonardo da Vinci and Albert Einstein are examples of such great designers (although I don't believe they ever took the MBTI).

Great designers have a large set of standard patterns that they apply to each new problem. If the problem fits an existing pattern, the great designer can easily solve it using a familiar technique.

Great designers have mastery of the tools they use.

Great designers aren't afraid of complexity, and some of the best are drawn to it. But their goal is to make the seemingly complex simple. As Einstein said, everything should be made as simple as possible, but no simpler. The French writer and aircraft designer Antoine de Saint-Exupéry made much the same point when he said, "You know you have achieved perfection in design not when you have nothing more to add, but when you have nothing more to take away."

Great designers seek out criticism of their work. The feedback loop that criticism supports allows them to try and discard many possible solutions.

Great designers usually have experience on failed projects and have made a point of learning from their failures. They try out and discard more alternatives. They are often wrong, but they discover and correct their mistakes quickly. They have the tenacity to continue trying alternatives even after others have given up.

They are not afraid of using brute force to solve a problem. Thomas Edison worked on the problem of designing a filament for an electric light bulb for nearly two years, and he tried thousands of materials. An assistant once asked him how he could keep trying after failing so many times. Edison didn't understand the question. In his mind, he hadn't failed at all. He is supposed to have replied, "What failure? I know thousands of things that do not work."

Great designers must be creative to generate numerous candidate design solutions. A great deal of research has been done on creativity, and there are some common themes. Creative people are curious, and their curiosity covers a wide range of interests. They have high energy. They are self-confident and independent enough to explore ideas that other people think are foolish. They value their own judgment. They are intellectually honest, which helps them differentiate what they really think from what the conventional wisdom says they should think.

Great designers have a restless desire to *create*—to make things. That desire might be to create a building, an electronic circuit, or a computer program. They have a bias toward action. Great designers aren't satisfied merely to learn facts; they feel compelled to *apply* what they have learned to real-world situations. To the great designer, not applying knowledge is tantamount to not having obtained the knowledge in the first place.

Programmers live for the "aha" insights that produce breakthrough design solutions. I think this is one of the reasons software developers' affinity for Monty Python makes more sense than it might at first appear. Monty Python flouts social conventions using unorthodox juxtapositions of elements of time and culture. The same independent-minded, out-of-the-box thinking that gives rise to Monty Python's scripts can also give rise to the innovative technical design solutions that programmers strive for.

Some of these characteristics match the programmer stereotype, and some do not. People outside software development might think of computer programming as dry and uncreative. People inside software development know that some of the most exciting projects of our times could not be accomplished without extreme software creativity. Movie animation, space exploration, computer games, medical technology—it's hard to find a leading-edge area that doesn't depend on software developers' creativity.

Software developers know that, stereotypes aside, computer programming gives them a medium in which they can create something out of nothing. That provides them with the same satisfaction that others obtain from sculpting, painting, writing, or other activities that are more obviously creative. "Mind-numbingly boring?" I think not.

Total and Absolute Commitment

The stereotype of the programmer working 12 to 16 hours at a time contains more than a grain of truth. To be an effective developer, you need to be able to concentrate exclusively on the programming task. That concentration exacts a penalty. While concentrating on a programming project, you lose track of time. One morning you look up, and it's 2:00 p.m. You've missed lunch. One Friday evening you look up, and it's 11:00 p.m. You've stood up your date or neglected to tell your spouse you were coming home late. One October you look up and realize that the summer is over and you missed it again because you've spent the past three months concentrating on an interesting project.

The Pony Express ad at the beginning of the chapter could be applied to some of today's software developers. It can be hard to have a family, friends, or other social ties when you work as much as some software developers do. Here is Pascal Zachary's description of programmer commitment on the Windows NT project:

> Work pervades their existence. Friends fade into the background. The ties of marriage fray or rip apart. Children are neglected or deferred. Hobbies wither. Computer code comes to mean everything. If private dreams are nursed at all, it is only to ease the pain of creating NT.[12]

At the end of the NT project, some developers left the company. Some were so burned out that they left the software field entirely.

Recognizing this phenomenon, some experienced developers have difficulty signing up for new projects because they know that in so doing they will once again choose to lose evenings, weekends, and summers.

This pattern is avoidable by moving to an engineering approach to software development. The average project spends 40 to 80 percent of its time correcting defects.[13] With software engineering, the team doesn't create the defects in the first place or it positions itself to eliminate the defects more quickly and easily. Eliminating 50 percent of the work is one quick way to reduce the workweek from 80 hours to 40.

Developers' high task completion need creates an unusual relationship between their commitment to their projects and their commitments to their companies. In my experience, no matter how much software developers dislike their companies, they rarely quit in mid-project. Workers in other fields would say, "I hate my company. I'm going to wait until right in the middle of the project, then quit. That'll show them!" Software developers say, "I hate my company. I'm going to finish this project to show the company what they're losing, then I'll quit. That'll show them!"

Programmers also seem committed to their occupation. One difficulty companies have in enforcing nondisclosure agreements is that many programmers feel more loyal to their colleagues at other companies than they do to their own employers. I have observed that software developers routinely discuss company confidential material with colleagues who are not covered by nondisclosure agreements. In their judgment, the free exchange of information between companies is more important than any one specific company's protection of its trade secrets. Programmers in the Open Source movement apply the idea more broadly and advocate that all source code and related materials should be disclosed for the public good.[14]

I think this loyalty to a project, tendency to work long hours, and high need for creativity are all related. Once a programmer has visualized the software to be built, bringing the vision to life becomes paramount, and the programmer feels tremendously unsettled until that can be done.

This ability to make a strong commitment to a vision bodes well for the establishment of a profession of software engineering. Programmers have a desire to commit to something beyond themselves—to their colleagues on a project or to other colleagues industry-wide. A profession of software engineering and its related professional societies can provide a constructive focus for this occupational commitment.

Software Demographics

The stereotype of programmers as young men appears to have some merit too. The average software worker is significantly younger than the United States labor force. As Figure 7-1 shows, the age structure of the software workforce peaks at about 30 to 35 years old, which is about 10 years younger than the peak for other types of technical workers.

The majority of software developers are male. In the latest year for which data is available (2000), 72 percent of computer and information science bachelor degrees and 83 percent of the Ph.D.s were awarded to men.[15] In high school, only 17 percent of people taking the advanced placement test for computer science are female, which is the lowest of any subject.[16]

Programmers are younger than average and tend to be male. The comparison to Pony Express riders begins to look less and less like an exaggeration (though there's no evidence that computer programmers are any more "wiry" than average).

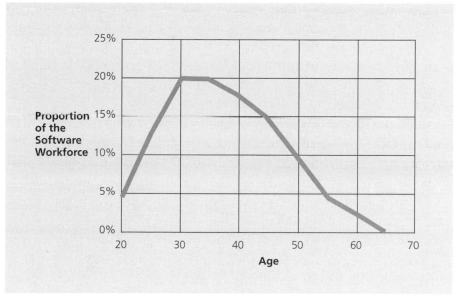

FIGURE 7-1

The biggest group of software workers is 30 to 35, which is about 10 years younger than the biggest groups of workers in other technical occupations.

Source: "A Moving Target: Studies Try to Define the IT Workforce"[17]

Education

Most programmers go through a gradual occupational awakening. When I wrote my first small programs, I thought, "Once I get the program to compile and quit getting all these syntax errors, I'll have computer programming figured out." After I stopped having problems with syntax errors, sometimes my programs still didn't work, and the problems that were left seemed even harder to figure out than the syntax errors were. I adopted a new belief, "Once I get the program debugged, I'll have computer programming figured out." That worked until I started creating larger programs and began to have problems because the various pieces I created didn't work together the way I thought they would. I came to rest on a new belief, "Once I figure out how to design effectively, I'll finally have software development figured out." I created some beautiful designs, but then some of my designs had to change because the requirements kept changing. At that point, I thought, "Once I figure out how to get good requirements, I'll finally have software development figured out." Somewhere along the path to learning how to get good requirements I began to realize that I might *never* get software development figured out. That realization was my first real step toward software engineering enlightenment.

Programmers take many circuitous paths to personal enlightenment, some resembling mine, and some different. Most developers are well-educated in general but self-taught about software development. As Table 7-1 shows, about 60 percent of software developers have obtained bachelor's degrees or higher. According to the United Engineering Foundation, about 40 percent of all software workers obtained their degrees in software-related disciplines.[18] About half of those who eventually obtained a software-related degree did so after first obtaining a bachelor's degree in some other subject. Another 20 percent of all software workers obtained degrees in subjects such as mathematics, engineering, English, history, or philosophy. The remaining 40 percent completed high school or some college but did not obtain a four-year degree.

Universities in the United States currently award about 35,000 computer science and related degrees per year[19] while about 50,000 new software development jobs are created each year.

The implication of all these statistics is that a great many software developers have not received any systematic training in computer science,

TABLE 7-1
Software developer education[20]

HIGHEST LEVEL OF EDUCATION ATTAINED	PERCENT OF SOFTWARE DEVELOPERS
High school graduate or equivalent or less	11.8
Some college, no degree	17.2
Associate's degree	11.0
Bachelor's degree	47.4
Graduate degree	12.8

much less in software engineering. What education they have obtained has been acquired through on-the-job training or self-study. Providing more consistent education in software engineering represents a significant opportunity to improve the level of software development practices.

Job Prospects

The total current employment for software workers in the United States is about two million. As Table 7-2 shows, jobs are divided among computer scientists, computer programmers, systems analysts, network analysts, and software engineers. (Some of these government-statistic job titles might sound old fashioned, but they do include modern software jobs.)

Job prospects for software developers in the United States are very good. According to the Bureau of Labor Statistics, computer and data processing services will be the fastest growing industry from 2000 to 2010, with a projected increase of 86 percent during this period. Software engineering is expected to be the fastest growing job category overall. All computer-related job categories are expected to increase.[21]

TABLE 7-2
Job breakdown for software workers[22]

JOB TITLE	CURRENT NUMBER OF SOFTWARE PERSONNEL IN THE U.S.
Computer and information scientists, research	28,000
Computer programmers	585,000
Computer software engineers, applications	380,000
Computer software engineers, systems software	317,000
Computer systems analysts	431,000
Network systems and data communications analysts	119,000
Other computer specialists	203,000
Total	2,063,000

TABLE 7-3

Software development jobs worldwide[23]

YEAR	TOTAL PROGRAMMERS
1950	100
1960	10,000
1970	100,000
1980	2,000,000
1990	7,000,000
2000	10,000,000
2010	14,000,000
2020	21,000,000

Worldwide, software development jobs are expected to increase as dramatically as they are increasing in the United States. Table 7-3 shows the projected increase.

With a 15,000-job-per-year gap between baccalaureate degrees awarded and jobs created, demand for computer programmers should remain high in the United States for at least the next several years, despite cyclical ups and downs in the job market. Labor shortages have been a perennial feature of the software world at least since the mid-1960s.[24] Software-related jobs are rated well in terms of salary, benefits, work environment, job stress, job security, and other factors.[25] Programmers know that, desirable as their jobs are, there isn't much competition for them.

Programming Heroes and Ball Hogs

Combine a shortage of skilled workers with the common tendency to set overly optimistic schedules, and the stage is set for the programming hero. Programming heroes take on challenging assignments and write mountains of code. They work vast amounts of overtime. They become indispensable to their projects. Success, it seems, rests squarely on their shoulders.

Project managers both love and fear hero programmers because they are smart, temperamental, and sometimes a little self-righteous, and because the managers don't see any way to complete the project without them.[26] In a tight labor market, replacing them isn't an option.

Unfortunately, the reality is that for every programming hero who is capable of monumental coding achievements, there are other pathological programming disasters who just don't know how to work well with others. They hoard design information and source code. They refuse to participate in technical reviews. They refuse to follow standards established by the team. The sum total of their actions is to prevent other team members from making potentially valuable contributions. A significant number of programming heroes don't turn out to be heroes at all; they turn out to be prima donna programming ball hogs.

Individual heroics can contribute to project success, but teamwork generally contributes more than individual accomplishment does. A study at IBM found that the average programmer spends only about 30 percent of the time working alone.[27] The rest is spent working with teammates, with customers, and on other interactive activities. Another study of 31 software projects found that the greatest single contributor to overall productivity was team cohesiveness.[28] Individual capabilities also significantly influenced productivity but were less influential than team cohesiveness.

Many people like to take on challenging projects that stretch their capabilities. Those who can test their limits, follow sound software development practices, and still cooperate with their teammates are the true programming heroes.

Cult of Personality

Upon examination, many aspects of the programmer personality stereotypes turn out to be accurate. The worker shortage contributes to increased hours for all workers who can be found—heroes and others—which means less time for those workers' self-education and professional development. This gives rise to a chicken-and-egg problem: We can't implement better development practices until we find the time for education and training, and we can't find the time for education and training until we implement better practices.

Working in favor of greater software professionalism is the fact that programmers are getting older. The longer the software field exists, the more the average age of working programmers will begin to match the age of the rest of the working population. The extreme personal sacrifices that are tolerable to young workers in their 20s become harder to justify as we become married, have children, become homeowners, and move into our 30s, 40s, 50s, and 60s. As the current cohort of programmers ages, the present hero-based approach to software development may naturally give way to approaches that rely more on working smart than on working hard. More software workers will adopt practices that allow them to complete their projects as promised and still be home in time for dinner.

Notes

1. *The Seattle Times,* October 8, 1995. Emphasis in original.

2. *USA Today,* February 16, 1998, pp. 1B–2B.

3. Bronson, Po, "Manager's Journal," *The Wall Street Journal,* February 9, 1998.

4. "Software Jobs Go Begging," *The New York Times,* January 13, 1998, p. A1.

5. Krantz, Les, *Jobs Rated Almanac,* NY: St. Martin's Press, 1999.

6. Thomsett, Rob, "Effective Project Teams: A Dilemma, a Model, a Solution," *American Programmer,* July–August 1990, pp. 25–35. Lyons, Michael L., "The DP Psyche," *Datamation,* August 15, 1985, pp. 103–109.

7. Thomsett, Rob, "Effective Project Teams: A Dilemma, a Model, a Solution," *American Programmer,* July–August 1990, pp. 25–35. Lyons, Michael L., "The DP Psyche," *Datamation,* August 15, 1985, pp. 103–109. Bostrom, R. P., and K. M. Kaiser, "Personality Differences within Systems Project Teams," *Proceedings of the 18th Annual Computer Personnel Research Conference,* ACM No. 443810, 1981.

8. Thomsett, Rob, "Effective Project Teams: A Dilemma, a Model, a Solution," *American Programmer,* July–August 1990, pp. 25–35. Lyons, Michael L., "The DP Psyche," *Datamation,* August 15, 1985, pp. 103–109.

9. National Center for Education Statistics, *2001 Digest of Educational Statistics,* Document Number NCES 2002130, April 2002.

10. Thomsett, Rob, "Effective Project Teams: A Dilemma, a Model, a Solution," *American Programmer,* July–August 1990, pp. 25–35. Lyons, Michael L., "The DP Psyche,"

Datamation, August 15, 1985, pp. 103–109. Bostrom, R. P., and K. M. Kaiser, "Personality Differences within Systems Project Teams," *Proceedings of the 18th Annual Computer Personnel Research Conference,* ACM No. 443810, 1981.

11. Glass, Robert L., *Software Creativity,* Englewood Cliffs, NJ: Prentice Hall PTR, 1994.

12. Zachary, Pascal, *Showstopper!: The Breakneck Race to Create Windows NT and the Next Generation at Microsoft,* New York: Free Press, 1994.

13. Software Engineering Institute, quoted in Fishman, Charles, "They Write the Right Stuff," *Fast Company,* December 1996. Mills, Harlan D., *Software Productivity,* Boston, MA: Little, Brown, 1983, pp. 71–81. Wheeler, David, Bill Brykczynski, and Reginald Meeson, *Software Inspection: An Industry Best Practice,* Los Alamitos, CA: IEEE Computer Society Press, 1996. Jones, Capers, *Programming Productivity,* New York: McGraw-Hill, 1986. Boehm, Barry W., "Improving Software Productivity," *IEEE Computer,* September 1987, pp. 43–57.

14. See, for example, R.M. Stallman, "The GNU Manifesto," 1985, www.fsf.org/gnu/manifesto.html. Raymond, E.S., "Homesteading the Noosphere," 1998, www.catb.org /~esr/writings/homesteading.

15. National Center for Education Statistics, *2001 Digest of Educational Statistics,* Document Number NCES 2002130, April 2002.

16. "Software Jobs Go Begging," *The New York Times,* January 13, 1998, p. A1.

17. Lowell, Bill, and Angela Burgess, "A Moving Target: Studies Try to Define the IT Workforce," *IT Professional,* May/June 1999.

18. Lowell, Bill, and Angela Burgess, "A Moving Target: Studies Try to Define the IT Workforce," *IT Professional,* May/June 1999.

19. National Center for Education Statistics, *2001 Digest of Educational Statistics,* Document Number NCES 2002130, April 2002.

20. *Occupational Outlook Handbook 2002-03 Edition,* Bureau of Labor Statistics, 2002.

21. *Occupational Outlook Handbook 2002-03 Edition,* Bureau of Labor Statistics, 2002.

22. Hecker, Daniel E., "Occupational employment projections to 2010," *Monthly Labor Review,* November 2001, vol. 124, no. 11.

23. Jones, Capers, *Applied Software Measurement: Assuring Productivity and Quality,* 2d Ed., New York: McGraw-Hill, 1997.

24. Bylinsky, Gene, "Help Wanted: 50,000 Programmers," *Fortune,* March 1967, pp. 141ff.

25. Krantz, Les, *Jobs Rated Almanac,* NY: St. Martin's Press, 1999.

26. Bach, James, "Enough about Process: What We Need Are Heroes," *IEEE Software,* March 1995, pp. 96–98.

27. McCue, Gerald M., "IBM's Santa Teresa Laboratory—Architectural Design for Program Development," *IBM Systems Journal,* vol. 17, no. 1, 1978, pp. 4–25.

28. Lakhanpal, B., "Understanding the Factors Influencing the Performance of Software Development Groups: An Exploratory Group-Level Analysis," *Information and Software Technology,* 35 (8), 1993, pp. 468–473.

CHAPTER EIGHT

Raising Your Software Consciousness

*If a man will begin with certainties, he shall end in doubts;
but if he will be content to begin with doubts he shall end in
certainties.*

FRANCIS BACON

In 1970, Charles Reich published a best-selling book called *The Greening of America*.[1] In it, Reich identifies three kinds of awareness or consciousness, which he calls Consciousness I, Consciousness II, and Consciousness III.

Consciousness I ("Con I") is the pioneer mentality. People who operate at Con I place great value on independence and self-satisfaction. They don't easily tolerate other people telling them what to do. They are highly self-reliant and self-sufficient. Reich believes that Con I dominated the American psyche during America's first centuries and that this focus on self-reliance was a significant factor in America's development.

Consciousness II is the gray flannel suit mentality—corporation man. People who operate at Con II understand the importance of getting along with others and playing by the rules. They believe rules are good for society, and they think everyone should follow them. Reich believes that Con II became more dominant than Con I in the mid-twentieth century.

Consciousness III is the mentality of enlightened independence. The Con III person operates on the basis of principles, with little regard for the rules that predominate in Con II and without the selfishness that predominates in Con I. By the time *Greening* was published, Reich argued that

Con II's time was over. He believed Con III was in its ascendancy and would soon replace Con II.

Although *The Greening of America* struck a resonant chord when it was published, history has not been kind to the book. In 1999, *Slate* magazine's readers voted it the silliest book of the twentieth century. Reich's Con III was a hippie nirvana, and the "greening" Reich predicted was a nationwide movement toward the hippie culture of the 1960s and 1970s—psychedelic drugs, bell-bottom pants, and all. As the hippie culture faded into obscurity in the 1980s, so did the credibility of Reich's predictions.

Can't Get No Satisfaction

Reich's political predictions may not have withstood the test of time, but his classification of Con I, Con II, and Con III provides a useful model for the software industry today.

Con I in software is associated with a focus on *self-reliance.* Software experts often refer to software developers operating at this level of awareness as mavericks, cowboy programmers, Lone Rangers, and prima donnas. Software developers at this level tend to have little tolerance for other people's ideas. They like to work alone. They don't like following standards. The "Not Invented Here" syndrome thrives.

Con I's advantage is that little training is needed, and the lone wolf approach works adequately in environments that employ only small numbers of programmers who work independently on small projects. Con I's disadvantage is that it scales poorly to projects that need teams of programmers rather than isolated individuals, which means it is valuable only on the smallest projects.

Con II in software is associated with a focus on *rules.* Many software developers eventually discover the limitations of Con I's self-reliant development style and see the advantages of working in groups. Over time, they learn rules that allow them to coordinate their work with others. Some groups of developers create their own informal rules through trial and error, and these groups can be highly effective. Other groups buy a prebuilt methodology. Sometimes the rules are provided by consultants—as in the classic "17 three-ring-binders" methodologies. Other times, the rules are taken from books, such as the Rational Unified Process,[2] the Extreme Programming series,[3] or my own *Software Project Survival Guide.*[4] Developers at this level of awareness tend to focus on details of adherence to the rules. They argue about which interpretations of the rules are correct and focus on "following the methodology."

Con III in software is associated with a focus on *principles.* At this level of awareness, developers understand that the rules of any prepackaged methodology are, at best, approximations of principles. Those approximations might apply most of the time, but they won't apply all of the time. Extensive education and training are needed to introduce a developer to the Con III principles underlying effective software development, and that education and training is not easily obtained. Once that education and training has been obtained, however, the developer is equipped with a full range of software engineering tools to support success on a wide range of projects.

Whereas a Con II approach consists of the repetitive application of techniques and procedures, Con III's focus on principles requires the application of judgment and creativity. With Con II, a developer can be trained to use just a single approach. If a good approach is chosen, a developer can leverage a relatively small amount of training across many projects. The gap between Con II and Con III will appear to be small when a Con II approach is used within its area of applicability. But a Con II developer will be ill-equipped to succeed on projects that fall outside the range of the specific methodology in which the developer was trained. The Con II developer is essentially an individual example of the Cargo Cult organization described in Chapter 3—procedures are followed without a thorough understanding of what makes them work, which leads to spotty project results.

Love the One You're With

The software industry has a long history of trying and ultimately rejecting "one size fits all" methodologies. These methodologies are Con II software approaches, and they fail outside of narrowly defined areas of applicability—predictably—precisely because they are Con II. The world of software is far too varied to be addressed by a single set of rules.

For example, compare the practices you would use to develop a heart pacemaker control to those you would use to develop a video store management program. If a software malfunction caused you to lose one DVD out of 1,000, it might affect the store's profitability by a fraction of a percent, but the impact would be negligible. If a malfunction caused one pacemaker out of 1,000 to fail, however, you've got a real problem. Generally speaking, products that are widely distributed need to be developed more carefully than products that are narrowly distributed. Products whose reliability is important need to be developed more carefully than products whose reliability doesn't much matter.

These different kinds of software require different development practices. Practices that would be considered to be overly rigorous, bureaucratic, and cumbersome for a video store management software might be considered irresponsibly quick and dirty—or reckless—for an embedded pacemaker control. The Con III developer will use different practices to develop a heart pacemaker control than to develop an inventory tracking system for videos. The Con II developer will attempt to apply a one-size-fits-all methodology to both projects with the likelihood that the methodology won't work particularly well for either one.

Are You Experienced?

Reich identified the three levels of consciousness as the zeitgeists of different eras, but I see Con I, Con II, and Con III as three distinct steps along a path of personal software engineering maturity. Most software developers begin their careers at Con I and eventually journey to Con II. In some environments, Con II supports effective work, and no further development is needed. In many environments, however, a further progression toward Con III is needed.

The by-the-book methodologies of Con II seem to be a reasonable learning path for developers at Con I who are not yet well versed in a wide range of software practices. The specific details of the rules-based practices probably don't matter all that much. People who are trying to raise themselves from Con I to Con II simply need to take a first step away from the chaos of a completely unmanaged project. They need to learn a set of rules and acquire experience applying those rules before they can advance to the Con III level, at which they understand software project dynamics well enough to break the rules when needed. This whole process is part of the natural progression from apprentice to journeyman to master.

Notes

1. Reich, Charles, *The Greening of America,* New York: Random House, 1970.

2. Kruchten, Philippe, *The Rational Unified Process: An Introduction,* 2d Ed., Boston, MA: Addison-Wesley, 2000.

3. Beck, Kent, *Extreme Programming Explained: Embrace Change,* Reading, MA: Addison-Wesley, 1999.

4. McConnell, Steve, *Software Project Survival Guide,* Redmond, WA: Microsoft Press, 1998.

CHAPTER NINE

Building the Community

*If any human being earnestly desires to push on to new dis-
coveries instead of just retaining and using the old; to win
victories over Nature as a worker rather than over hostile
critics as a disputant; to attain, in fact, clear and demon-
strative knowledge instead of attractive and probable theory; we invite him as a true son of Science to join our ranks.*

FRANCIS BACON

In 1984, I started my first full-time programming job as an analyst for
a consulting firm with about five employees. The job paid well. We
got free diet Pepsi. And I got to work on IBM PC projects, which were
a lot more interesting than the mainframe projects I'd been working on
in school.

The projects were much larger than my school projects, lasting anywhere
from a day to a month. I learned a set of skills that I hadn't learned in
school. I learned to coordinate my work with others. I learned to contend
with a boss who constantly changed his mind about each project's requirements. And I learned to work with customers who depended on the software and actually complained if it didn't work the way they needed it to.

My second job was on a large mainframe aerospace project—a stereotypical document-laden government project. The inefficiency was astound-
ing. I was convinced that three or four of the programmers from my old
company could have written in three months what this 30-person project
team took three or four years to create. (I still think that's probably true.)

One of the people on the project had a copy of Niklaus Wirth's *Algorithms + Data Structures = Programs,*[1] and he was regarded as the project guru, from all appearances largely because he had read this one book. I didn't like this job very much, and by the time I left work each day, I happily stopped thinking about computer programming.

After the aerospace project, I went back to working in a small company environment as the only programmer in the office. I began work on an exciting year-long DOS shrink-wrap project in C that pushed the PC to its limits. This project didn't provide free diet Pepsi, but I was happy to be working with microcomputers again. The only hitch was that the new project had renewed my excitement for computer programming, and I couldn't find anyone else who was as excited about computer programming as I was.

By this time I had been working full time in the industry about three years and, aside from programming language and machine manuals, I hadn't yet read any programming books or subscribed to any programming magazines. (Though I had bought a copy of *Algorithms + Data Structures = Programs.*)

The small company I was working for presented itself to the public as "The A Team" of programmers. I was told during my job interview that the company had a lot of trade secrets that enabled it to be "The A Team." After I started, I said I wanted to learn the "trade secrets," and my boss handed me a copy of Philip Metzger's *Managing a Programming Project.*[2] I read the book immediately, and was amazed to find that Metzger seemed to have had many of the same experiences I had been having. I had struggled with the planning for my new year-long DOS project. Metzger's book cleared up many of my problems, and I used it as a basis for the planning I did for the rest of that project.

Shortly after reading *Managing a Programming Project,* I found a copy of Ed Yourdon and Larry Constantine's *Structured Design*[3]. In skimming it, I saw an explanation of why I was having such a hard time with the design for my DOS program. I inverted my module calling hierarchy, as Yourdon and Constantine suggested, and the whole design fell into place. I started to realize that there might be more information available to help me do my job well than I had previously realized.

About this time I foggily recalled some letters my professors had mentioned a few years earlier: A-C-M and I-E-E-E. I didn't have a computer programming degree and didn't feel like a professional programmer, but I decided to apply for membership anyway. I began receiving *Communications of the ACM*,[4] *IEEE Computer*,[5] and *IEEE Software*.[6] *IEEE Software* quickly became my favorite. I discovered articles that addressed the issues I needed to learn about to do my job more effectively: how to help customers make up their minds about requirements; how to control complexity on large projects; how to create maintainable code; how to coordinate the work of multiple programmers; and so on. The articles weren't as fluffy as the articles in some of the popular magazines I was reading, and I felt they might even help me throughout my career.

This was a watershed event in my growth as a software developer. Prior to joining the community of *IEEE Software* readers, I had viewed programming as just a job. I went to work. I got paid. I went home. I stopped thinking about software. After joining the *IEEE Software* community, I began to see that, even if I worked in an office by myself, I wasn't just a lone programmer. I was part of a community of software developers who cared about software development and took the time to share their experiences for the benefit of other software developers.

Considering the extreme variation in education and skill levels in the software world, a person could argue that there currently isn't any meaningful software development community, but I think this variation makes it all the more important to build one. Every community is made up of some more skilled and some less skilled practitioners. A community must address the needs of both young and old practitioners. It must address the needs of practitioners with strong educational backgrounds in computer science, software engineering, and related topics, but also of self-taught programmers—scientists, engineers, accountants, teachers, doctors, attorneys, and others—who find that they are now writing programs for a living, even though they never consciously set out to become software developers or software engineers.

Professional associations such as the IEEE Computer Society are an important part of any mature profession. They provide opportunities for like-minded professionals to congregate, exchange ideas in person, in books, in articles, in interest groups, and at conferences. Professional organizations support numerous structured ways of exchanging the valuable tips and tricks of the trade that software engineers need to be on the A Team.

Notes

1. Wirth, Niklaus. Algorithms + Data Structures, Englewood Cliffs, NJ: Prentice-Hall, 1985.

2. Metzger, Philip W., *Managing a Programming Project,* 2d Ed., Englewood Cliffs, NJ: Prentice Hall, 1981. This book is now available as Metzger, Philip W., and John Boddie, *Managing a Programming Project,* 3d Ed., Upper Saddle River, NJ: Prentice Hall PTR, 1996.

3. Yourdon, Edward and Larry L. Constantine. Structured Design: Fundamentals of a Discipline of Computer Program and Systems Design, Englewood Cliffs, NJ: Yourdon Press, 1979.

4. See www.acm.org.

5. See www.computer.org/computer.

6. See www.computer.org/software.

CHAPTER TEN

Architects and Carpenters

Engineers produce plans. Builders implement the plans to produce a product.

TERRI MAGINNIS

W ithin mature fields, occupations are both stratified and specialized. In the construction industry, architects and engineers produce the plans that are built by general contractors. General contractors typically subcontract parts of a job to specialty contractors such as framers, plumbers, electricians, and landscapers. The software industry is developing its own stratification into software architects and carpenters. It's also developing its own specializations into software framers, plumbers, electricians, and landscapers.

Job Stratification

In other disciplines, professional engineers are supported by engineering technicians and technologists. The National Institute for Certification in Engineering Technologies offers five kinds of certification for them. We see similar stratification in medicine with doctors, physicians' assistants, registered nurses, licensed practical nurses, and nurses aides. In law, you see attorneys, paralegals, and legal secretaries. Complex fields become stratified.

As Figure 10-1 illustrates, as software engineering becomes more mature, software occupations will stratify into jobs that require greater amounts of

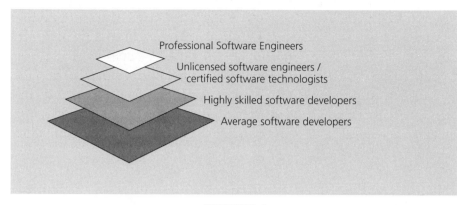

FIGURE 10-1

The software development field is stratifying into different levels of professional standing. The most highly trained software workers will generally command the most responsibility and the highest salaries.

education and training and those that require lesser amounts. Some software developers will obtain a comprehensive education in professional software engineering; others will learn computer programming as a craft. Of the developers who receive a software engineering education, some will go on to obtain their Professional Software Engineering licenses, but most will not. Those who obtain their licenses will be the occupational equivalent of physicians, while those who receive a comprehensive education but do not obtain full professional standing will become the occupational equivalent of physician's assistants.

Eventually, we'll also see separate credentials for software engineers and software technologists—today's coders. Software technologists will become the occupational equivalent of a physician's assistant or registered nurse in medicine or certified technologist in engineering. Some software technologists will seek out certification, and some will not. In general, the jobs that require more education and training will command more responsibility and greater prestige—just as they do in other professions.

Software developers who pursue top professional credentials will probably be compensated better than other software developers. The average person who obtains a professional degree in the United States earns at least 50 percent more than the average person who obtains only a bachelor's degree.[1] The average person who obtains a master's degree earns 25 percent more than the average person who obtains only a bachelor's degree. And the gap is likely to widen. The Bureau of Labor Statistics reports that from 2000 to 2010 demand will increase 11 percent for occupations requiring moderate on-the-job training up to 23 percent for occupations requiring a master's degree.[2]

Job Specialization

In addition to stratification, the software industry needs to define job specializations. Most software workers today are generalists. One moment they're architects; the next moment they're high-tech carpenters, pounding in code one line at a time. Specialization is an important element of a mature profession.

Twenty-five years ago, Fred Brooks proposed one kind of software engineering specialization when he suggested that programming teams be structured using a surgical team model. One chief programmer (the "surgeon") would write nearly all of the code, and other team members would be arrayed around the chief programmer in well-defined support roles.[3] A test project in the late 1960s in which a team was structured this way demonstrated unprecedented productivity,[4] and Brooks thought the surgical team structure was responsible for the project's results.

Applying an additional quarter century of hindsight to this extraordinary project, it seems that its remarkable productivity might not have arisen from the specific surgical team structure but from the project's high degree of specialization. Studies about other software engineering practices have found that good training in specialty roles contributes more to effectiveness than the use of a particular practice does.[5]

In the software industry today, two categories of specializations are emerging: technology specialization and software engineering specialization. As Figure 10-2 suggests, software technologists will specialize primarily

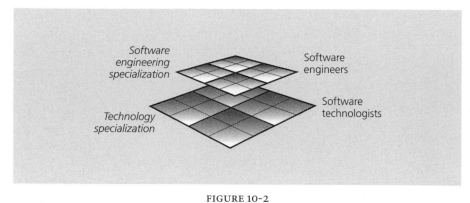

FIGURE 10-2

In addition to its stratification, the software field is developing many different technol-ogy specialties and software engineering specialties.

on the basis of their knowledge of specific technologies. Various "software technologist" certifications are already available from specific companies such as Microsoft, Novell, Oracle, and Apple Computer.

Specialization is also beginning to occur in software engineering practices, and this is an important trend. Capers Jones estimates that lack of software engineering specialization is currently causing low quality, schedule delays, and cost overruns in about 90 percent of all United States software organizations.[6]

As Table 10-1 suggests, the more software workers a company employs, the greater its need for specialists—people whose job focuses primarily on a specialty area rather than general programming. In a small organization of ten software employees, all ten employees might be generalists, or there might be a relatively simple distinction between development, test, and management. In the small number of large organizations that employ 10,000 software workers, at least 20 percent of the employees will be specialists, and in some organizations specialization can run as high as 40 percent. Jones has encountered more than 100 different specializations in his organizational assessment work.

The specific specializations shown in this table are rough averages. The ratios of specialists to generalists will vary among different companies and different kinds of software organizations.

TABLE 10-1

Appropriate specializations by company size[7]

SPECIALTY	NUMBER OF SOFTWARE EMPLOYEES				RATIO TO GENERALISTS
	<10	<100	<1,000	≈10,000	
Proportion of Specialists	0%	10–25%	15–35%	20–40%	—
Architecture			X	X	1 : 75
Configuration control			X	X	1 : 30
Cost estimating			X	X	1 : 100
Customer support		X	X	X	1 : 25*
Database administration		X	X	X	1 : 25
Education and training				X	1 : 250
Function point counting			X	X	1 : 50
Human factors				X	1 : 250*
Information systems				X	1 : 250*
Integration				X	1 : 50
Maintenance and enhancement	O	X	X	X	1 : 4
Measurement			X	X	1 : 50
Network		X	X	X	1 : 50
Package acquisition				X	1 : 150
Performance				X	1 : 75
Planning				X	1 : 250*
Process improvement				X	1 : 200
Quality assurance	O	X	X	X	1 : 25
Requirements			X	X	1 : 50*
Reusability				X	1 : 100
Standards				X	1 : 300
Systems software support		X	X	X	1 : 30
Technical writing	O	X	X	X	1 : 15
Testing	O	X	X	X	1 : 8
Tool development				X	1 : 250*

*This value was estimated based on Jones's discussion, but he doesn't give a specific value for this specialization.

O—Occasionally observed; X—Usually observed.

The benefits of specialization are not unique to software. A country doctor in practice for himself has to be a generalist, but large urban hospitals employ hundreds of specialists. Professional engineers take specialty exams, as do attorneys. Specialization is an attribute of a mature field.

Team Specializations

Individual projects need specialization as much as organizations do. My company has created a technical project organization, based on the SWE-BOK knowledge areas described in Chapter 5, that includes the following specialists on even our smallest projects:

- Construction lead
- Design lead
- Planning and tracking lead
- Project business manager
- Quality assurance lead
- Requirements lead

On most projects, these lead roles are part-time responsibilities, but we've found it useful to have a specific person assigned to look out for a project's interests in each of these areas. Each area requires specialized knowledge on even a five to ten person project. More information on these lead areas, including recommended study programs for each one, is available from my company's Web site at www.construx.com/profession.

Time Will Tell

Is increasing stratification and specialization a foregone conclusion, or will this prediction just look silly 20 years from now? Given sufficient time, my crystal ball says that software will become just as specialized and stratified as other mature fields. This has already happened in medicine, law, professional engineering, and other mature professions. Whether that stratification and specialization in software will take 10 years, 20 years, or longer, my crystal ball doesn't say.

Notes

1. National Center for Education Statistics, *2001 Digest of Educational Statistics,* Document Number NCES 2002130, April 2002.

2. *Occupational Outlook Handbook 2002-03 Edition,* Bureau of Labor Statistics, 2002.

3. Brooks, Frederick P., Jr., *The Mythical Man-Month,* Anniversary Edition, Reading, MA: Addison-Wesley, 1995.

4. Baker, F. Terry, "Chief Programmer Team Management of Production Programming," *IBM Systems Journal,* vol. 11, no. 1, 1972, pp. 56–73. Baker, F. Terry, and Harlan D. Mills, "Chief Programmer Teams," *Datamation,* Volume 19, Number 12 (December 1973), pp. 58–61.

5. Fred Brooks makes a similar point on page 257 of the 20th Anniversary Edition of *The Mythical Man-Month,* though he doesn't relate it back to the surgical team: "I came to insist that student teams as small as four people choose a manager and a separate architect. Defining distinct roles in such small teams may be a little extreme, but I have observed it to work well and to contribute to design success even for small teams."

6. Jones, Capers, *Assessment and Control of Software Risks,* Englewood Cliffs, NJ: Yourdon Press, 1994.

7. Adapted from Jones, Capers, *Assessment and Control of Software Risks,* Englewood Cliffs, NJ: Yourdon Press, 1994, and Jones, Capers, *Patterns of Software Systems Failure and Success,* Boston, MA: International Thomson Computer Press, 1996.

CHAPTER ELEVEN

Programmer & Writing

*Read not to contradict and confute, nor to believe and take
for granted, nor to find talk and discourse, but to weigh and
consider.*

FRANCIS BACON

In 1987, Fred Brooks observed that "the gap between the best software engineering practice and the average practice is very wide—perhaps wider than in any other engineering discipline. A tool that disseminates good practice would be important."[1] Continuing Brooks's line of thought in 1990, the Computer Science and Technology Board stated that the biggest gains in software development quality and productivity will come from disseminating effective practices—codifying, unifying, and distributing existing knowledge in the form of software engineering handbooks.[2]

Who should write these handbooks?

In August 1837, Ralph Waldo Emerson delivered an address that came to be known as "The American Scholar." One hundred and sixty-five years later, I believe it contains the answer to the question of who should write these software handbooks.

As the software book publishing industry is currently configured, most software development books are written by six kinds of authors:

- Recent retirees
- University professors

- Seminar instructors
- Consultants
- Think-tank developers
- Developers working on production software

People in each of these groups have valuable contributions to make, and it would be a mistake to discount any of them. Recent retirees bring years of experience, insight, and reflection to their writing. University professors bring a full awareness of leading-edge research. Seminar instructors have a chance to test their material in front of hundreds of students before publishing their material in book form. Consultants see dozens of clients a year, and their observations can be based on an incredible breadth of exposure to effective and ineffective software practices. Think-tank developers at Xerox PARC, AT&T Labs, and similar environments have produced some of our best software engineering technology. But I think that developers working on production software must shoulder the primary burden of creating these handbooks.

In "The American Scholar," Emerson draws a distinction between a thinker and Man Thinking (which is his synonym for American Scholar). A thinker is someone whose sole function is to think. A thinker experiences life second-hand, through other people's books, articles, and descriptions of the active world. A Man Thinking, on the other hand, is a robust person who is active in the world, actively engaged in a trade or occupation, who occasionally pauses for reflection. The Man Thinking has a strong bias toward action. "The true scholar grudges every opportunity of action past by as a loss of power. It is the raw material out of which the intellect molds her splendid products." Emerson argues that the direct experience of Man Thinking is critical to genius, and that genius can emanate only from a Man Thinking, not from a mere thinker.

Emerson says that immersion in the active world is essential to understanding what other Men Thinking have written about it. The reader who does not bring a base of action to his reading will understand little of what he reads. But, "When the mind is braced by labor and invention, the page of whatever book we read becomes luminous with manifold allusion.

Every sentence is doubly significant and the sense of our author is as broad as the world."

If readers not "braced by labor and invention" get little out of what they read, writers not braced by labor and invention put little into what they write. As Emerson says, action is essential. Without it, thought can never ripen into truth. Readers instantly know whose words are loaded with life, and whose are not. "I learn immediately from any speaker how much he has already lived, through the poverty or the splendor of his speech. Life lies behind us as the quarry from whence we get tiles and copestones for the masonry of today. . . . Colleges and books only copy the language which the field and the work-yard made."

I call thinkers not being able to write authentically the James Fenimore Cooper syndrome. Cooper was an early American writer who was fascinated by the American Indians and wrote several stories about them including *The Deerslayer* and *The Last of the Mohicans.* Cooper's writing was later skewered by the great American humorist Mark Twain as being hopelessly inaccurate fantasy.[3]

In a scene from *The Deerslayer,* Cooper has six Indians climb onto a sapling overhanging a river to wait for a scow being hauled upstream by rope. The Indians' plan is to jump onto the roof of a cabin on the scow that is 90 feet long and 16 feet wide in the middle of the scow. The six Indians precisely time their jumps onto the cabin roof, but one falls short of the roof and lands on the boat's stern; the remaining five miss the boat entirely and land in the water.

Twain had been a riverboat pilot, and he took Cooper to task for his sloppy description of a subject Twain knew intimately. Twain pointed out the implausibility of a "sapling" being able to support the weight of six adult men. He then pointed out that according to Cooper's description of the river, a scow one-third the length of Cooper's scow would have had difficulty navigating the twists and turns in the river; Cooper's scow would have wedged itself into a corner halfway through the first turn. As for the Indians jumping, the maximum speed the scow could be pulled upstream was about one mile per hour, which would have given the Indians a minute and a half to jump onto the boat, and a full minute to jump onto the roof of the cabin. That amount of time hardly calls for precise timing, but Cooper's Indians managed to miss the cabin anyway. Perhaps they lost their concentration when they realized that Cooper's river was only two feet wider than Cooper's boat at the point it passed the Indians' location; they could have saved themselves some trouble by simply stepping onto the boat from the shore as it scraped past them, but, as Twain says, Cooper didn't allow his Indians to hop on from the shore, and their mishap is his fault, not theirs.

At the 17th International Conference on Software Engineering, David Parnas pointed out that the papers from earlier conferences that had received awards for being "most influential" had arguably not been influential at all.[4] I think the James Fenimore Cooper syndrome is part of the reason. These papers might influence researchers, but they do not influence practitioners because, to practitioners, the methodologies they describe seem about as authentic as Cooper's Indians.

Practicing software developers are every bit as skeptical about software development handbooks as Twain was of Cooper's prose. Software methodology books are seen as theoretical, applicable only to small projects, hard to adapt, inefficient, and incomplete. Software authors sometimes bemoan the fact that the average software developer buys less than one software development book a year, but I do not think the reason for that is such a great mystery. Developers will buy books that have been "braced by labor and invention," but not books that, like Cooper's Indians, miss the boat.

Mark Twain argued that the best frontier adventure stories are written by people with keen eyes for detail who had actually lived on the frontier, and I am convinced that the best software handbooks will be based on the work of software developers who have recently lived through production software projects. To apply Emerson's point to software engineering, the tiles and copestones of software engineering handbooks must come from the Programmer Writing, from people who are actively participating on production software projects and who occasionally take time to reflect on their work and write about it.

If you are actively developing software, I urge you to write about your insights. If you have worked on a project that taught you valuable lessons, share them—whether they are coding details, quality assurance practices, more effective project management, or even a software development topic that doesn't have a name yet. Submit your writing to a magazine, or fully develop your ideas into a book. If your insights are stronger than your writing, find a consultant, seminar instructor, university professor, or other skilled writer to be your co-author. You don't need to worry that what you have learned won't apply to other people's projects. As Emerson says, "Success treads on every right step. For the instinct is sure, that prompts him to tell his brother what he thinks. He then learns that in going down into the secrets of his own mind he has descended into the secrets of all minds. . . . The deeper he dives into his privatest secretest presentiment, to his wonder he finds this is the most acceptable, most public, and universally true."[5]

Notes

1. Brooks, Fred, "No Silver Bullets—Essence and Accidents of Software Engineering," *Computer,* April 1987.

2. "Scaling Up: A Research Agenda for Software Engineering," *Communications of the ACM,* March 1990.

3. Twain, Mark, "Fenimore Cooper's Literary Offenses," 1895.

4. Parnas, David, "On ICSE's 'Most Influential' Papers," *Software Engineering Notes,* July 1995.

5. Selections from Ralph Waldo Emerson, Edited by Stephen E. Whicher. Boston, MA: Houghton Mifflin Company, 1960.

PART THREE

Organizational Professionalism

CHAPTER TWELVE

Software Gold Rushes

Prosperity doth best discover vice, but adversity doth best discover virtue.

FRANCIS BACON

The root of all superstition is that men observe when a thing hits, but not when it misses.

FRANCIS BACON

In January 1848, James Marshall discovered gold in California's American River near a mill he was building for John Sutter. At first Marshall and Sutter dismissed the pea-sized nuggets as a nuisance; they believed the attention that gold would bring would spoil Sutter's plans to build an agricultural empire. But within months word spread, and by 1849 thousands of men and a handful of women from around the world had contracted Gold Rush Fever. They headed to California to make their fortunes in what became known as the California Gold Rush. The rush west created a new economy driven by high-risk entrepreneurialism and fueled by dreams of striking it rich. Precious few 49ers actually realized that dream during the gold rush days, but the dream lives on in many modern software companies and individual software developers.

The California Gold Rush was unique in that the gold was found in riverbeds instead of embedded in hard rock. That meant that, at first, anyone with a tin pan and an entrepreneurial spirit had a chance to make a fortune. But by mid-1849, most of the easy gold had been found, which meant that a typical miner spent ten hours a day in ice cold water, digging, sifting, and washing. As time passed, this backbreaking work yielded less and less gold. There were occasional lucky strikes well into the 1850s, which provided just enough good news to encourage thousands to keep digging. Most failed every day, but they kept on for years.

After the early days of the gold rush, miners had to use more advanced techniques to extract gold. By the early 1850s, a single miner could no longer work a claim by himself. He needed the help of other people and technology. At first, miners banded together informally to build dams, reroute rivers, and extract the gold. But soon more capital-intensive techniques were needed, and the informal groups of miners were replaced by corporations. By the mid-1850s, most of the miners who remained were corporate employees rather than individual entrepreneurs.

Software Gold Rushes

The advent of a major new technology often means the beginning of what I think of as a "software gold rush." Companies and individual entrepreneurs rush into new technology areas, hoping that a little bit of hard work will produce a product that will make them wealthy. I've personally seen software gold rushes with the advent of the IBM PC and Microsoft DOS operating system, the migration from DOS to Windows, and the growth of Internet computing. More new-technology gold rushes will undoubtedly follow.

Gold rush software development is characterized by high-risk, high-reward development practices. Few companies have established competitive presences in the marketplace during the early days of a new technology, and many of the new-technology gold nuggets—successful new products—seem to be lying on the ground, waiting for anyone with the right mix of innovation and initiative to pick them up. Software 49ers rush into the new technology, hoping to stake their claim before anyone else does. The typical gold rushers are two guys working in a garage, legendary dynamic duos such as Bill Gates and Paul Allen of Microsoft, Steve Jobs and Steve Wozniak of Apple Computer, and Bob Frankston and Dan Bricklin of VisiCalc.

The practices employed by software developers with gold rush fever are usually associated with hacking rather than engineering: informal processes, long hours, little documentation, bare-bones quality assurance practices—in other words, hero-based code-and-fix development. These practices require little training and low overhead, and they expose projects to a high risk of failure.

The odds of striking it rich during a software gold rush are about as good as they were during the California Gold Rush—for every success story, there are hundreds of projects that go bust. But these small failures aren't nearly as interesting as the huge successes, and so we don't hear very much about them. Two guys who work hard and don't strike it rich aren't a very good news story, unless by chance there's something interesting about their garage.

As with the California Gold Rush, software projects run with hero-based development in gold rush periods are successful from time to time. The gold rush projects are so enormously lucrative when they do succeed that they convince software developers that high-risk practices can work, and thus the rare but widely publicized successes spread Gold Rush Fever and help to keep hero-based practices alive.

Post-Gold Rush Development

Post-gold rush software development is characterized by more methodical, lower-risk, more capital-intensive, more labor-intensive development practices. Projects use larger teams, rely on more formal processes, adhere to more standards (compatibility with legacy code, industry-wide protocols, and so on), and work with much larger code bases. The emphasis is less on rushing software to market quickly and more on reliability, interoperability, and usability. Projects focus on software engineering considerations that hardly matter during a gold rush but that matter a lot after a technology matures.

Gold rush-style development practices have even lower odds of working in a post-gold rush phase than they did during the risky gold rush phase. In the early days of a new technology, there are few established players or products. The technological barriers to entry are low, and early products can be small, unpolished, and unreliable and still succeed. As with the California Gold Rush, fewer people and less capital are needed to stake a claim during the early days of a new technology. The first version of Word for the Macintosh was a gold rush product that consisted of just 153,000 lines of code. Two guys in a garage have a chance to compete against the major corporations when a successful product can be built with 153,000 lines of code. As the technology matures, however, the easy gold runs out, and successful companies have to compete on the basis of more capital-intensive projects.

One of the most damaging mistakes that successful gold rush companies make is to persist in using gold rush development approaches as the technology matures and their projects scale up. To compete successfully in the post-gold rush phase, the successful project needs to do a lot more than simply multiply the number of guys and get a bigger garage.

Post-gold rush customers are more demanding. Gold rush customers are what Everett M. Rogers, author of *Diffusion of Innovations,* calls "Innovators" and "Early Adopters."[1] They tend to be technologically savvy, drawn to new technologies, and forgiving of the rough edges that go along with them. Gold rush products can be much less polished than the products that come later and still be successful. Post-gold rush customers are what Rogers calls "Early Majority," "Late Majority," and "Laggards." They are risk averse and want polished products that work reliably. This demand sets a higher bar for post-gold rush products. The current version of Word for Windows, a post-gold rush product, consists of more than 5,000,000 lines of code.

One surprising implication of gold rush dynamics is that the companies that are successful during one gold rush are likely to fail during the next gold rush. The archetypal post-gold rushers are the companies that became established during an earlier gold rush. These companies repeat Marshall and Sutter's mistake of seeing new-technology gold as a nuisance that will interfere with their well-laid plans for extracting maximum value from the claims they staked during the last gold rush. Examples of companies that were slow to pick up new-technology gold nuggets include IBM during the early days of PC-DOS; Lotus during the early days of Windows;

and Microsoft during the early dawn of the Internet, although Microsoft recovered from its early mistakes. The most compelling example in modern computing has to be Xerox. Many of the fundamental ideas of modern desktop computing were invented at Xerox's Palo Alto Research Center, including the GUI interface, the mouse, and the Ethernet. But Xerox was so busy trying not to lose the copy machine war that it lost the computing war without ever really entering it.

Other post-gold rush companies are just too bloated to compete effectively in gold rush markets. The overhead necessary to sell to Early Majority and Late Majority customers isn't needed during a gold rush. In a gold rush market, you can cut your products to the bone and still do well with the innovators and early adopters who count the most in those markets.

We'll undoubtedly see this boom and bust pattern repeated during whatever technology cycle follows the Internet. Some of the companies that had the greatest successes in the early days of the Internet—such as Amazon.com, eBay, and Yahoo—will miss the next wave; only time will tell which will successfully navigate the next great transition.

The Sense and Nonsense of Gold Rush Economics

From a macroeconomic viewpoint, thousands of individual software developers taking on entrepreneurial risk voluntarily—with a few lucky entrepreneurs striking it rich and the rest chalking up their losses to experience—is tremendously beneficial. No one but the individual entrepreneur pays for the failures, and everyone has a chance to benefit from buying and using the few products that succeed. But how can an individual company harness this dynamic? What company could possibly afford to fund thousands of individual entrepreneurs during a gold rush phase just to find the one or two that successfully develop new gold rush technology? Even companies with extensive research facilities like AT&T, IBM, Microsoft, and Xerox can't afford to fund thousands of projects in each new technology area, which is one reason that software company acquisitions during a gold rush phase are more sensible than they at first appear.

Some industry observers thought Microsoft was crazy to pay $130 million to acquire Vermeer Technology, original creators of FrontPage, when Vermeer had only about $10 million in annual revenue. But from the entrepreneurial gold rush point of view, paying $130 million for the one success in a thousand is a cheap alternative to funding a thousand internal dead-end entrepreneurial experiments.

Scaling Up and Scaling Down

Post-gold rush software engineering practices have unequivocally proved their worth on large projects. (Doubters can turn to Chapters 13 and 14.) They also have a lot to offer smaller projects. Larry Constantine describes an Australian Computer Society Software Challenge in which three-person teams had to develop and deliver a 200 function-point application in six hours.[2] This is a significant challenge, equivalent to writing about 20,000 lines of code in a traditional third-generation language or about 5,000 lines of code in a visual programming language.

A team from Ernst and Young decided to follow a formal development methodology—a scaled-down version of their regular methodology—complete with staged activities and intermediate deliverables. Their approach included careful requirements analysis and design. Many of their competitors dived straight into coding, and for the first couple of hours the team from Ernst and Young lagged behind.

But by mid-day they had developed a commanding lead. At the end of the day the team from Ernst and Young lost, but not because their systematic approach had failed. They lost because they accidentally overwrote some of their working files, squandering their afternoon work and delivering less functionality at the end of the day than they had demonstrated at lunchtime.

Would the team from Ernst and Young have won without the configuration-management snafu? The answer is yes. They reappeared a few months later at another rapid-development face-off—this time with version control and backup—and they won.[3] Their success was achieved not by stripping down their earlier approach but by identifying weaknesses in their old process and making improvements.

This general value of applying systematic process improvement within small organizations has been confirmed by a Software Engineering Institute study.[4] The success rate of process improvement programs in organizations with fewer than 50 software developers has been just as good as it has been in larger organizations. Moreover, small organizations have fewer of the problems that inhibited success in larger organizations, such as organizational politics and turf guarding.

Back to the Gold Rush

Gold rush software projects are inherently risky, but the use of haphazard software development practices has unnecessarily added even more risk. Developers working on gold rush projects have been saddled for decades with the methodological equivalents of tin pans and shovels. The result is that many of their insights, ideas, and innovations are needlessly lost, just as the Ernst and Young team's work was needlessly lost due to lack of source code control.

Systematic approaches to software engineering are necessary for post-gold rush projects to succeed; they are equally useful for projects still in the gold rush stage. What would have happened if the original designers of VisiCalc, Lotus 1-2-3, MacOS, the Mosaic Web browser, and other groundbreaking products had overwritten their working files? How many innovative products have we never heard of because their developers *did* overwrite their working files? And how many have succumbed to more subtle errors?

During a gold rush, you can be terribly sloppy and not very skilled and still make a fortune, but the odds are against you. After a gold rush, you have to be more disciplined and more skilled just to break even. The entrepreneurial buzz a person gets from participating in a gold rush project is one of life's great thrills, but there's no conflict between entrepreneurial energy and the use of effective software development practices. By examining the practices that work well in post-gold rush environments, you can gain insights into practices that work best when you have Gold Rush Fever, increasing your chances of ultimately hitting pay dirt.

Notes

1. Rogers, Everett M., *Diffusion of Innovations,* 4th Ed., New York: The Free Press, 1995.

2. Constantine, Larry, "Under Pressure," *Software Development,* October 1995, pp. 111–112.

3. Constantine, Larry, "Re: Architecture," *Software Development,* January 1996, pp. 87–88.

4. Herbsleb, James, et al., "Software Quality and the Capability Maturity Model," *Communications of the ACM,* June 1997, pp. 30–40.

CHAPTER THIRTEEN

Business Case for Better Software Practices

When you can measure what you are speaking about, and
express it in numbers, you know something about it; but
when you cannot measure it, when you cannot express it in
numbers, your knowledge is of a meager and unsatisfactory
kind.

LORD KELVIN, 1893

Companies that invest in post-gold rush development practices have found that their investments pay off. In 1994, James Herbsleb reported that the average "business value" (roughly the same as return on investment) for 13 organizations that had taken on systematic improvement programs was about 500 percent, with the best organizations realizing returns of 900 percent.[1] In 1995, Neil C. Olsen reported similar returns for organizations that had made significant investments in staffing, training, and work environments.[2] In 1997, Rini van Solingen reported that the average ROI was 700 percent with the best organization realizing returns of 1,900 percent.[3] In 2000, Capers Jones reported that the return on investment from process improvement could easily go into double digits (i.e., go higher than 1000 percent).[4] A recent analysis by Watts Humphrey found that the ROI for improved software practices could be in the neighborhood of 500 percent or better.[5]

State of the Practice

Most people probably assume that software organizational effectiveness is distributed according to a typical bell curve—a few really poor organizations, a few exceptional organizations, and the majority somewhere in the middle. This is shown in Figure 13-1.

Contrary to the expectation, the reality is quite different. Due to the slow uptake of effective software practices, as discussed in Chapters 1 and 2, only a handful of organizations are operating at the highest levels. Industry researchers have long observed a tremendous disparity between the best and worst organizations operating within the same industries—on the order of 10 to 1.[6] The average organization is much closer to the least effective organizations than to the best, as shown in Figure 13-2.

The implication of this distribution is that most software personnel have never seen software development at its best. This gives rise to skepticism about whether things are really better anywhere. Even people who have worked in the software industry for 20 or 30 years might never have seen software development at its best. Most of them have spent their entire careers working in organizations to the left side of Figure 13-2. But, as the

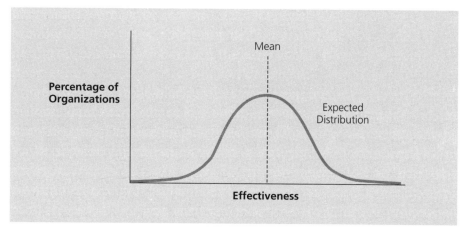

FIGURE 13-1
Most people expect organizational effectiveness to be symmetrically distributed, with an equal number of effective and ineffective software organizations.

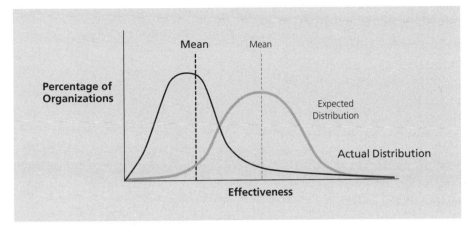

FIGURE 13-2

The actual distribution of software effectiveness is asymmetric. Most organizations perform much closer to the worst practice than to the best.[7]

data in this chapter shows, the best organizations are indeed much better than the average.

Detailed Benefits of Improved Software Practices

An in-depth study of 13 organizations by the Software Engineering Institute found that the typical (median) organization engaged in systematic improvement experienced a productivity gain of 35 percent per year, schedule reduction of 19 percent per year, and reduction in post-release defect reports of 39 percent per year. These gains provided the underpinnings for the overall returns on investment. These results are summarized in Table 13-1.

The gains experienced by the best organizations were even better. The organization with the strongest productivity gains improved 58 percent per year over a 4-year period, for a total compounded gain of more than 500 percent. The best schedule reduction was 23 percent per year for 6 years, for a total compounded schedule reduction of 91 percent. The best long-term quality improvement was a reduction in post-release defect reports of 39 percent per year for 9 years, for a total compounded defect

TABLE 13-1
Results of software process improvement efforts[8]

FACTOR	MEDIAN IMPROVEMENT	BEST SUSTAINED IMPROVEMENT
Productivity	35%/year	58%/year
Schedule	19%/year	23%/year
Post-release defect reports	39%/year	39%/year*
Business value of organizational improvement	500 percent	880 percent

*The "median" and "sustained" values here are the same because the highest defect-reduction results were short-term and not counted as "sustained" improvements.

reduction of 99 percent. Two organizations achieved short-term defect reductions of 70 percent or more in less than 2 years.

Organizations that are hooked on code-and-fix development tend to think there is a tradeoff between low defect count and productivity. But as I explained in Chapter 2, much of the cost on a code-and-fix project arises from unplanned defect-correction work. The results in Table 13-1 confirm that for most organizations no tradeoff exists between higher productivity and better quality. Organizations that focus on preventing defects also get shorter schedules and higher productivity.

As a percentage, the number of companies that have engaged in systematically improving their software practices is small. In raw numbers, hundreds of organizations have engaged in systematic improvement, and many have reported their results in professional journals, conference proceedings, and other publications. Table 13-2 summarizes the returns on investment reported by 20 organizations.

TABLE 13-2
Examples of software improvement ROI[9]

ORGANIZATION	RESULTS
BDN International	ROI 300%
Boeing Information Systems	Estimates within 20%, $5.5 million saved in 1 year, ROI 775%

TABLE 13-2 *continued*

ORGANIZATION	RESULTS
Computer Sciences Corporation	65% reduction in error rates
General Dynamics Decision Systems	70% reduction in rework; 94% defect rate reduction; 2.9 × productivity gain
Harris ISD DPL	90% defect rate reduction; 2.5 × productivity gain
Hewlett-Packard SESD	ROI 900%
Hughes	$2 million annual reduction in cost overruns, ROI 500%
IBM Toronto	90% reduction in delivered defects, 80% reduction in rework
Motorola GED	2–3 × productivity improvement, 2–7 × cycle time reduction, ROI 677%
Philips	ROI 750%
Raytheon	ROI 770%
Schlumberger	4 × reduction in beta test bugs
Siemens	90% reduction in released defects
Telcordia	Defects 1/10 industry average, customer satisfaction increased from 60% to 91% over 4 years
Texas Instruments—Systems Group	90% reduction in delivered defects
Thomson CSF	ROI 360%
U.S. Navy	ROI 410%
USAF Ogden Air Logistics Center	ROI 1,900%
USAF Oklahoma City Air Logistics Center	ROI 635%
USAF Tinker Air Force Base	ROI 600%

ROIs for Selected Practices

Details of how organizations have achieved their greater software development effectiveness vary among different organizations. Nonetheless, some specific practices have been found to be generally effective. Table 13-3 shows the ballpark ROIs for a few selected practices.

TABLE 13-3
Return on investment for selected software practices[10]

PRACTICE	12-MONTH ROI	36-MONTH ROI
Formal code inspections	250%	1,200%
Formal design inspections	350%	1,000%
Long-range technology planning	100%	1,000%
Cost and quality estimation tools	250%	1,200%
Productivity measurements	150%	600%
Process assessments	150%	600%
Management training	120%	550%
Technical staff training	90%	550%

Insights from Software Estimation

The accuracy of an organization's estimates is a good indicator of how well it manages and executes its projects. A Standish Group survey of more than 26,000 business systems projects found that the average project overran its planned budget by more than 100 percent.[11] The level of estimation error reported in this survey is consistent with other industry findings.[12]

Figure 13-3 shows one finding from a study of United States Air Force projects at different levels of software practices. (This analysis is based on the SW-CMM, which I'll discuss more in Chapter 14.) Each point below 100 percent represents a project that finished under budget. Each point above 100 percent represents a project that overran its estimate.

As you can see from Figure 13-3, the least sophisticated projects (SW-CMM Level 1) routinely overran their projects' budgets—in other words, they routinely underestimated their projects' costs. More sophisticated organizations (at SW-CMM Level 2) spread their estimation error more evenly between overestimation and underestimation, but the relative error of the estimates was still commonly 100 percent or more. For the most sophisticated organizations (those at SW-CMM Level 3), overruns and underruns become equally common, and the estimation accuracy became much improved.

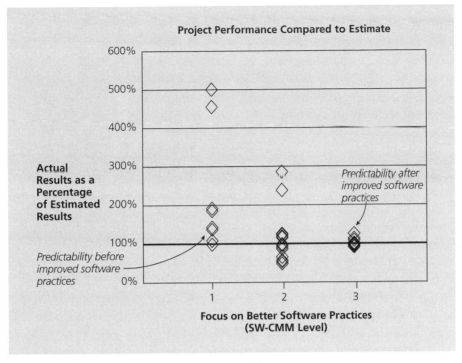

FIGURE 13-3

As organizations improve their software practices, they gain more control over their project estimates, which is generally indicative of better project control.[13]

Indirect Benefits of Improved Software Practices

The return on investment figures in the published literature have mostly been based on operational savings, that is, on reducing development cost per line of code written or per function point delivered. While these savings are impressive, the greater business benefit might arise from the significant *indirect* returns attributable to improved software practices. Better software practices improve cost and schedule predictability, reduce risk of cost and schedule overruns, provide early warnings of problems, and support better management.

For a software products company, what is the business value of improving schedule estimation accuracy from ±100 percent to ±10 percent? What is the value of being able to make a commitment to customers 6 to 12 months in advance of a scheduled completion date with high confidence of delivering on that commitment? For a company that develops custom software, what is the business value of being able to provide a fixed-price bid with high confidence that the project will not significantly overrun the bid? For a retail sales organization, what is the value of being able to plan cutover to a new system with pinpoint accuracy? What is the value of knowing with confidence that cutover will occur October 1, as planned, with little risk of running into the holiday sales season?

Unlike the operational benefits that most of the industry literature has focused on, the indirect benefits of improved software practices open the door to additional revenue opportunities. For top decision makers, these indirect benefits may be more compelling than the direct, cost-savings benefit.

A View of the Best

Further examination of estimation practices holds out an interesting process-improvement carrot. Most organizations find that as their projects become larger, each team member becomes less productive. In contrast with the economies of scale experienced in other kinds of work, software projects usually experience *dis*economies of scale.

Organizations that use systematic estimation practices use formulas like this one to estimate their software project effort:[14]

$$\textbf{Effort} = \textbf{2.94} \times \textbf{KSLOC}^{1.10}$$

Effort is the number of staff-months and *KSLOC* is the estimated number of lines of code in thousands. The numbers 2.94 and 1.10 are derived by calibration using data from projects that the organization has already completed. The values of 2.94 and 1.10 apply to typical organizations. The specific value of the exponent (1.10) is significant because it means that larger projects require disproportionately more effort than smaller projects.

NASA's Software Engineering Laboratory (SEL) is a notable exception. The SEL was the first organization to receive the IEEE's award for software process achievement and is one of the most sophisticated software development organizations in the world. The SEL uses the following formula to estimate effort on its projects:[15]

$$\text{Effort} = 1.27 \times \text{KSLOC}^{0.986}$$

In spite of its small type, the exponent of 0.986 points to a momentous difference between the SEL's formula and the formulas used by every other software organization. Every other published estimation model uses an exponent greater than 1.0. The fact that the SEL's exponent is less than 1.0 suggests that the SEL is achieving a slight *economy* of scale. The process improvement carrot this represents is that sufficiently mature organizations might be able to turn the large-project problem on its head. They might actually be able to improve per-person productivity slightly as their projects grow larger. Although rare, this is indeed a logical consequence of the specialization I discussed in Chapter 10.

Challenge Is Organizational

Many organizations push responsibility for improved software practices down to the project level. As I was reviewing the "effort-multiplier" factors in the popular Cocomo II estimation model[16] recently, I was struck by how few factors are under the control of an individual project manager. Of the 22 factors Cocomo II uses to fine-tune a project's base effort estimate, only three in my judgment are typically under the control of an individual project manager (the factors of Level of Documentation, Architecture and Risk Resolution, and Development for Reuse). Numerous factors are dictated by the nature of a company's business (product complexity, required reliability, platform volatility, unprecedentedness of the software, and so on). These factors cannot easily be changed without changing businesses. The remaining factors cannot readily be influenced by individual projects and must be addressed by the organization—staff capability, multi-site development, personnel continuity, process maturity, and other factors. These organization-level areas seem to be where the greatest leverage for improved software practices lies.

The Last Great Frontier

For a typical business-investment decision, the desirability of the investment is determined by weighing the return on investment against the cost of capital. An investment that produces a return greater than the cost of capital—all things considered—will be a good investment.[17] (This is a simplified explanation. See the citations for more complete explanations.)

Cost of capital is typically around 10 percent. In many business contexts, an investment with a return of 15 percent or 20 percent would be considered compelling. Improved software practices, however, do not offer returns of 15 percent or 20 percent. *According to the examples in Table 13-2 (as well as studies cited at the beginning of the chapter), improved software practices provide returns ranging from 300 percent to 1,900 percent and average about 500 percent.* Investments with these levels of returns are extraordinary—virtually unprecedented in business. These returns are higher than Internet stocks in the late 1990s. They're higher than successful speculation in the commodities markets. They're almost as good as winning the lottery, and they represent an unrivaled opportunity for any business that isn't already using these practices.

The reason for these exceptionally high returns is tied directly to the discussions in Chapters 1 and 2—improved practices have been available for decades, but most organizations aren't taking advantage of them. Risk of adopting these practices is low; payoff is high. All that's needed is the organizational resolve to use them.

Ten Tough Questions

As Lord Kelvin wrote more than 100 years ago, decision-making is difficult without quantitative data to support the decisions. Many organizations find they cannot answer basic questions about their software activities like these:

1. How much are you spending on software development?
2. What percentage of your projects are currently on time and on budget?

3. What is the average schedule and budget overrun for your projects?

4. Which of your current projects are most likely to fail outright?

5. What percentage of your project cost arises from avoidable rework?

6. How satisfied (quantitatively) are users of your software?

7. How do the skills of your staff compare to industry averages?

8. How do the capabilities of your organization compare to similar organizations?

9. How much (quantitatively) has your productivity improved in the past 12 months?

10. What is your plan for improving the skills of your staff and the effectiveness of your organization?

Organizations that cannot answer these questions almost certainly fall to the left side of Figure 13-2. Many organizations have never asked questions such as these and are only vaguely aware that they should be asking such questions. Considering that the business case for better software practices is so compelling, perhaps the 11th tough question should be, "What's keeping us from using better software practices now that we have seen this data?"

Notes

1. Herbsleb, James, et al., "Benefits of CMM Based Software Process Improvement: Initial Results," Pittsburgh: Software Engineering Institute, Document CMU/SEI-94-TR-13, August 1994.

2. Olsen, Neil C., "Survival of the Fastest: Improving Service Velocity," *IEEE Software*, September 1995, pp. 28–38.

3. van Solingen, Rini, "The Cost and Benefits of Software Process Improvement," *Proceedings of the Eighth European Conference on Information Technology Evaluation, September 17–18, 2001.*

4. Jones, Capers, *Software Assessments, Benchmarks, and Best Practices*, Boston, MA: Addison-Wesley, 2000.

5. Humphrey, Watts, *Winning with Software: An Executive Strategy*, Boston, MA: Addison-Wesley, 2001.

6. Mills, Harlan D., *Software Productivity,* Boston, MA: Little, Brown, 1983.

7. "Process Maturity Profile of the Software Community 2001 Year End Update," Software Engineering Institute, March 2002.

8. Data in this table is from Herbsleb, James, et al., "Benefits of CMM Based Software Process Improvement: Initial Results," Pittsburgh: Software Engineering Institute, Document CMU/SEI-94-TR-13, August 1994.

9. Adapted from Krasner, Herb, "Accumulating the Body of Evidence for the Payoff of Software Process Improvement—1997," November 19, 1997 (unpublished paper). van Solingen, Rini, "The Cost and Benefits of Software Process Improvement," *Proceedings of the Eighth European Conference on Information Technology Evaluation, September 17-18, 2001.* Diaz, Michale, and Jeff King, "How CMM Impacts Quality, Productivity, Rework, and the Bottom Line," *CrossTalk,* vol. 15, no. 3 (March 2002), pp. 9–14.

10. Jones, Capers, *Assessment and Control of Software Risks,* Englewood Cliffs, NJ: Yourdon Press, 1994.

11. The Standish Group, "Charting the Seas of Information Technology," Dennis, MA: The Standish Group, 1994. Johnson, Jim, "Turning Chaos into Success," *Software Magazine,* December 1999, pp. 30–39 (Johnson is Chairman of The Standish Group).

12. See, for example, Capers, Jones, *Patterns of Software Systems Failure and Success,* Boston, MA: International Thomson Computer Press, 1996.

13. Lawlis, Dr. Patricia K., Capt. Robert M. Flowe, and Capt. James B. Thordahl, "A Correlational Study of the CMM and Software Development Performance," *Crosstalk,* September 1995.

14. See, for example, Boehm, Barry, et al., *Software Cost Estimation with Cocomo II,* Boston, MA: Addison-Wesley, 2000, which contains the coefficient of 2.94, its baseline coefficient, and the exponent of 1.10 as the nominal exponent.

15. NASA Software Engineering Laboratory, *Software Engineering Laboratory (SEL) Relationships, Models, and Management Rules,* Document Number SEL-91-001, Greenbelt, MD: Goddard Space Flight Center, NASA, 1991.

16. Boehm, Barry, et al., *Software Cost Estimation with Cocomo II,* Boston, MA: Addison-Wesley, 2000.

17. Fetzer, Daniel T., "Making Investment Decisions for Software Process Improvement," *DACS Software Tech News,* November 2002, pp. 19–22. Also available at www.dacs.dtic.mil/awareness/newsletters. Reifer, Donald J., *Making the Software Business Case: Improvement by the Numbers,* Boston, MA: Addison-Wesley, 2001.

CHAPTER FOURTEEN

Ptolemaic Reasoning

All models are wrong; some models are useful.
GEORGE BOX

Knowledge itself is power.
FRANCIS BACON

A few years ago I gave a talk titled "A Tale of Two Projects." My objective was to provide a glimpse of what an engineering approach to software development looks like. I argued that good software organizations often succeed on complex, high-risk projects because they use effective software development practices, while poor organizations often fail on simple, low-risk projects because they use poor practices. The talk was generally well received, but one person's evaluation said this: "An excellent example of the kind of static, linear, Ptolemaic reasoning that ignores the dynamics and complexities of real software projects."

In case you've forgotten your grammar school science, Ptolemy was an astronomer who lived about 100 A.D. and believed that the sun revolved around the earth. His theory was replaced in 1543 when Copernicus theorized that the earth revolved around the sun. The attendee was saying that the approach I recommended was a sun-moves-around-the-earth approach—either that, or that my ideas were 400 years out of date!

Copernicus replaced Ptolemy's theory when he discovered observational data that Ptolemy's theory could not account for. Similarly, data from real-world software projects strongly supports the efficacy of the engineering-oriented development practices I described, this attendee's particular comments notwithstanding.

Overview of SW-CMM

The practices I was describing were loosely based on the Capability Maturity Model for Software (SW-CMM), developed by the Software Engineering Institute (SEI). The SW-CMM was originally proposed in 1987 and is currently the best known and most effective approach to systematic software organization improvement. It represents the path most frequently traveled to achieve the business case benefits described in Chapter 13.

The SW-CMM classifies software organizations into five levels:[1]

Level 1: Initial. Software development is chaotic. Projects tend to run over budget and behind schedule. Organizational knowledge is contained only in the minds of individual programmers; when a programmer leaves an organization, so does the knowledge. Success depends largely on the contributions of individual "hero" programmers of the kind described in Chapter 7. These organizations tend to use code-and-fix development. Organizations are at this level by default unless they've deliberately adopted more effective approaches.

Level 2: Repeatable. Basic project management practices are established on a project-by-project basis, and the organization ensures that they are followed. Project success no longer depends solely on specific individuals. The strength of an organization at this level depends on its repeated experience with similar projects. The organization may falter when faced with new tools, methods, or kinds of software.

Level 3: Defined. The software organization adopts standardized technical and management processes across the organization, and individual projects tailor the standard process to their specific needs. A group within the organization is assigned responsibility for software process activities. The organization establishes a training program to ensure that managers and technical staff have appropriate knowledge and skills to work at this level. These organizations have moved well beyond code-and-fix development, and they routinely deliver software on time and within budget.

Level 4: Managed. Project outcomes are highly predictable. The process is stable enough that causes of variation can be identified and addressed. The organization collects project data in an organization-wide database to evaluate the effectiveness of different processes. All projects follow organization-wide process-measurement standards so that the data they produce can be meaningfully analyzed and compared.

Level 5: Optimizing. The focus of the whole organization is on continuous, proactive identification and dissemination of process improvements. The organization varies its processes, measures the results of the variations, and diffuses beneficial variations as new standards. The organization's quality assurance focus is on defect prevention through identification and elimination of root causes.

The underlying principle of the SW-CMM can be attributed loosely to Conway's Law: The structure of a computer program reflects the structure of the organization that built it.[2] Chaotic organizations produce chaotic software. Organizations that hire programming heroes, give them lots of autonomy, and set them loose to create coding miracles produce software that is alternately brilliant and erratic. Organizations bloated with inefficient processes produce piggy, sluggish software. And, presumably, efficient, optimizing organizations produce finely tuned, highly satisfactory software.

Moving Up

The software industry has been making progress under the guidance provided by the SW-CMM. As Figure 14-1 shows, in 1991, of 132 organizations assessed, only about 20 percent of organizations were performing at levels better than Level 1.[3]

As Figure 14-2 shows, in 2002, of 1,978 organizations assessed, more than two-thirds were performing at better than Level 1.

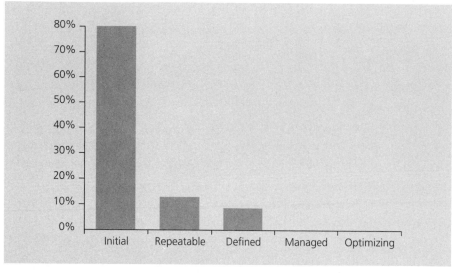

FIGURE 14-1

Assessment profile of organizations that have been assessed using the SW-CMM as of 1991.
Source: "Process Maturity Profile of the Software Community 2002 Year End Update."

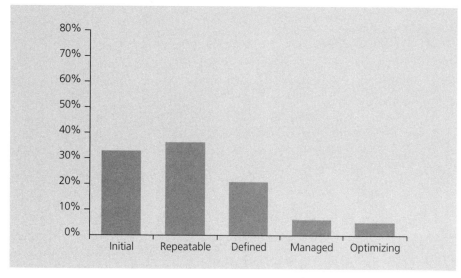

FIGURE 14-2

Assessment profile as of 2002.
Source: "Process Maturity Profile of the Software Community 2002 Year End Update."

The trend shown by these two graphs is encouraging, but only a small fraction of all the software organizations in North America have been assessed, and I think it's safe to assume that the profile of organizations overall still looks a lot more like the SEI's 1991 profile than its 2001 profile, in other words, that about 75 percent of all organizations are still operating at Level 1.[4]

Are these results attainable by average organizations? The answer is clearly yes. As Figure 14-3 shows, the SEI studied more than 300 organizations that were trying to improve their SW-CMM rating from Level 1 to Level 2 or from Level 2 to Level 3.[5] Seventy-five percent improved from Level 1 to Level 2 in three and one-half years or less, and the median time was 22 months. Seventy-five percent improved from Level 2 to Level 3 in two and one-half years or less, and the median time was about 21 months. Organizations that make a serious commitment to SW-CMM-style improvement typically improve substantially, and quickly too.

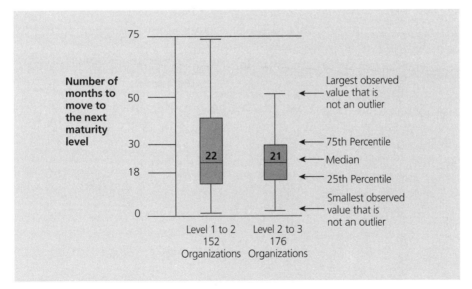

FIGURE 14-3

Experience of organizations in moving from one SW-CMM maturity level to the next since 1992.

Source: Adapted from "Process Maturity Profile of the Software Community 2002 Year End Update."

All the Risk You Can Handle

My Ptolemaic seminar attendee said my approach ignored the dynamics of real projects, and other people have claimed that the SW-CMM makes organizations risk averse.[6] They become bureaucratic and conservative, the claim goes, which hurts their competitiveness. How does the industry experience bear this out?

In Level 1 organizations, fewer than half the respondents to one survey said their management was willing to take on "moderate" or "substantial" risk. In Level 3 organizations, almost 80 percent said they were willing to take on that much risk.[7]

This relationship between process effectiveness and ability to take on risk was demonstrated by the Cheyenne Mountain ATAMS project.[8] The ATAMS project team committed to complete the project for one-fifth the cost and in one-half the time of the best available estimate. In the end, they delivered the software one month ahead of schedule and within budget. Eighteen months after release, only two defects had been discovered in the software, and both were easily corrected. The project team's success on this high-risk project resulted from carefully managing requirements, using formal inspections on their designs and code, and practicing active risk management.

The effect of organizational improvement on risk taking is the opposite of what some people think. By reducing exposure to unnecessary risks—the kind of risks Fred Brooks might call "accidental" rather than "essential"—the process-sophisticated organization is in a better position to take on calculated, voluntary risks than less sophisticated organizations, which are overwhelmed by involuntary risks assaulting them from all sides. (Chapter 5 contains a more detailed discussion of Brooks's distinction between accidental and essential properties.)

Who Uses the SW-CMM?

Since 1987, about 2,000 organizations have had their capabilities assessed, and more than 10,000 projects have had their results reported to the SEI.

Three-quarters of the organizations participating in SW-CMM improvement are commercial software houses or in-house development groups representing industries including finance, insurance, real estate, retail sales, construction, transportation, communications, public utilities, industrial machinery, electronic equipment, medical instruments, and many others. About a quarter develop software under contract for the United States government. About five percent are military organizations or government agencies. The organizations' sizes vary widely. About half have fewer than 100 software personnel. About a quarter have more than 200, and about a quarter have fewer than 50.

Soul-Less Software Development

One of the common objections to organizational improvement is that it imposes creativity-limiting bureaucracy. This is reminiscent of the old objection that engineering and art are incompatible. It is possible to create an oppressive environment in which programmer creativity and business goals are placed at odds, just as it is possible to create ugly buildings. But it is just as possible to set up an environment in which software developer satisfaction and business goals are in harmony, and industry data bears this out. Of people who were surveyed about the effects of the SW-CMM, 84 percent disagreed or strongly disagreed with the claim that SW-CMM-based improvement made their organizations more rigid or bureaucratic.

Organizations that have focused on organizational improvement have found that effective processes support creativity and morale. In a survey of about 50 organizations, only 20 percent of the people in Level 1 organizations rated their staff morale as "good" or "excellent."[9] The responses listed were consistent across managers, developers responsible for organizational improvement, and general senior technical staff members. In organizations rated at Level 2, the proportion of people who rated their staff morale as "good" or "excellent" jumped to 50 percent. And, in organizations rated at Level 3, 60 percent of the people rated their morale as "good" or "excellent."

These summary statistics are confirmed by in-depth analysis of organizations that have achieved the highest process effectiveness ratings. A survey at Ogden Air Logistics Center, one of the first organizations to be assessed at SW-CMM Level 5, found that software workers were enthusiastic about the changes brought about by their eight-year improvement effort.[10] Respondents did feel that the Level 5 processes constrained the way they could perform their work, but the constraint was seen as an inevitable side effect of becoming more effective and wasn't considered to be negative. Software workers felt that it was much easier to perform their work than it had been before organizational improvement. The vast majority felt that they had more input into project planning and control. Every survey respondent felt that the SW-CMM initiative had been a positive influence.

The on-board shuttle software group at NASA's Johnson Space Flight Center is another organization that has been assessed at Level 5.[11] You won't find mounds of pizza boxes, pyramids of Coca-Cola cans, rock-climbing walls, skateboard parks, or any of the other trappings found in more stylish software organizations. The emphasis is not on playing games; it is on making perfect software. The work is exciting, but it is not all-consuming. The space shuttle group generally works 8 to 5. In an industry dominated by males, about half of this software group is female.

People who leave such high-performance groups are sometimes shocked by how inefficient the average organization is. One person left the Johnson Space Flight Center for a more entrepreneurial environment, only to return a few months later. He commented that the company he went to paid lip service to developing software effectively, but their approach was really code-and-fix development. Far from finding high maturity environments limiting, people in those environments achieve levels of productivity and quality that are simply not possible in lower maturity environments. The ATAMS project described earlier used highly structured work practices that some developers might find restrictive, but the ATAMS team members said they felt the process brought out everyone's best performance. They said they would be reluctant to develop software without it.

Serious Commitment

One thing not to like is that organizational improvement isn't easy. James Herbsleb surveyed organizations that had performed SW-CMM improvement. Seventy-seven percent of respondents said that organizational improvement took longer than expected, and 68 percent said it cost more than expected.[12]

Succeeding at SW-CMM improvement depends on these factors:

- Commitment from top management, including providing leadership and funding, prioritizing long-term improvement as a high priority, and actively monitoring process-improvement progress.
- Establishment of a Software Engineering Process Group (SEPG). More than one SEPG may be required in a large organization. The SEPG must be staffed with senior people who understand the organization's improvement goals, the cultural issues involved in process improvement, and their roles as internal consultants.
- Appropriate training for middle management and technical staff, along with performance rewards that are aligned with long-term SW-CMM objectives.

This is a highly simplified list, and each specific organization will have additional specialized factors that will affect its improvement initiative. As I mentioned in Chapter 2, some organizations implement SW-CMM as a buzzword du jour. Attempts to treat the SW-CMM as yet another silver bullet are not likely to succeed.

Ratings for Organizations

The SW-CMM is a mature, effective model for organizational improvement. By stratifying software organizations into five levels, it is also an effective model for organizational assessment. Other, more mature professions use organizational assessment as part of their program for maintaining a high standard of practice. Accounting firms are required to go through a peer review every three years. Colleges are accredited for a maximum of three years and must be re-reviewed before their accreditation expires. Some individual programs within colleges are accredited separately. Hospitals are accredited by the Joint Commission on Accreditation of Healthcare Organizations (JCAHO) and are accredited for a maximum of three years.

JCAHO lists these reasons that a hospital would seek accreditation. Accreditation:[13]

- Enhances community confidence
- Provides a report card for the public
- Offers an objective evaluation of the organization's performance
- Stimulates the organization's quality improvement efforts
- Aids in professional staff recruitment
- Provides a staff education tool
- May be used to meet certain Medicare certification requirements
- Expedites third-party payment
- Often fulfills state licensure requirements
- May favorably influence liability insurance premiums
- Favorably influences managed care contract decisions

Hospital accreditation is a voluntary process, but most hospitals try to maintain accreditation for the reasons listed.

The parallels to software organizational assessment are clear. SW-CMM assessments provide a report card that potential clients can use in evaluating software contracting arrangements or packaged-software purchases. They provide an objective, publicly recognized standard of comparison. They stimulate quality improvement efforts by encouraging organizations to improve their level rankings. It's easy to imagine insurance companies providing better rates on errors and omissions policies to companies operating at higher maturity levels.

Form and Substance

There's an old saying that:

Success = Planning × Execution

If you assign a number between 0 percent and 100 percent to Planning and do the same for Execution, you will get a value for Success that ranges from 0 percent to 100 percent. If either planning or execution is missing, your chance of success will be 0 percent.

As the software industry moves toward higher levels of professionalism in software engineering, the great body of experience associated with the SW-CMM, both positive and negative, should be considered.

What is important about the SW-CMM is its substance, not its form. Organizations that focus on SW-CMM-style improvement solely for the sake of getting a "2" or "3" will likely have half-baked planning and half-hearted execution. They are unlikely to achieve either the numeric designation they want or the quality and productivity benefits they should want. This truly is Ptolemaic reasoning—letting the substance revolve around the form, instead of putting the substance at the center of the software solar system.

Organizations that focus on the bottom-line quality and productivity benefits offered by SW-CMM-style improvement are likely to take their planning more seriously and execute better. A focus on process allows organizations to become more productive, produce software with fewer defects, take on more risk, improve their estimates, raise morale, and perform better on large projects. Considering the level of effectiveness available to organizations that operate at a high level of process sophistication, it becomes clear that outdated practices like code-and-fix development are the real Ptolemaic reasoning.

Notes

1. The single best description of the SW-CMM is Carnegie Mellon University/ Software Engineering Institute, *The Capability Maturity Model: Guidelines for Improving the Software Process,* Reading, MA: Addison-Wesley, 1995. Other documents are available for download from the SEI's Web site at www.sei.cmu.edu.

2. Conway, M. E., "How Do Committees Invent?" *Datamation,* vol. 14, no. 4, 1968, pp. 28–31.

3. "Process Maturity Profile of the Software Community 2002 Year End Update," Software Engineering Institute, April 2003.

4. This is confirmed by Capers Jones, *Patterns of Software Systems Failure and Success,* Boston, MA: International Thomson Computer Press, 1996.

5. "Process Maturity Profile of the Software Community 2002 Year End Update," Software Engineering Institute, April 2003.

6. DeMarco, Tom, and Timothy Lister, *Peopleware: Productive Projects and Teams,* 2d Ed., New York: Dorset House, 1999.

7. Herbsleb, James, et al., "Software Quality and the Capability Maturity Model," *Communications of the ACM,* June 1997, pp. 30–40.

8. Gibbs, W. Wayt, "Command and Control: Inside a Hollowed-Out Mountain, Software Fiascoes—and a Signal Success," *Scientific American,* August 1997, pp. 33–34. Tackett, Buford D., III, and Buddy Van Doren, "Process Control for Error Free Software: A Software Success Story," *IEEE Software,* May 1999. Richard L. Randall, et al., "Product-Line Reuse Delivers a System for One-Fifth the Cost in One-Half the Time," *Crosstalk,* August 1996.

9. Herbsleb, James, et al., "Software Quality and the Capability Maturity Model," *Communications of the ACM,* June 1997, pp. 30–40.

10. Oldham, Leon G., et al., "Benefits Realized from Climbing the CMM Ladder," *Crosstalk,* May 1999.

11. Fishman, Charles, "They Write the Right Stuff," *Fast Company,* December 1996.

12. Herbsleb, James, et al., "Software Quality and the Capability Maturity Model," *Communications of the ACM,* June 1997, pp. 30–40. An "outlier" is a value that is more than 1.5 box lengths greater than the 75th percentile or more than 1.5 box lengths less than the 25th percentile.

13. See the JCAHO Web site www.jcaho.org.

CHAPTER FIFTEEN

Quantifying Personnel Factors

Personnel attributes and human relations activities provide by far the largest source of opportunity for improving software productivity.

BARRY W. BOEHM

A topic that sometimes gets lost in discussions of software best practices, process-improvement models, and other more complex topics is the role that soft, human-oriented factors play in software effectiveness.

Personnel Factors

One of the most replicated results in software engineering research is the significant productivity differences among individual software developers. In the first study on the subject, Sackman, Erikson, and Grant found differences of more than 20 to 1 in the time required by different developers to debug the same problem.[1] This was among a group of programmers who each had at least seven years of professional experience.

This basic result—demonstrating at least 10 to 1 differences in productivity—has been reproduced numerous times, but I think it understates the real productivity differences among practicing programmers. Tom DeMarco and Timothy Lister conducted a coding war game in which 166 programmers were asked to complete the same assignment.[2] They found that the different programmers exhibited differences in productivity of about 5 to 1 on the same small project.

In a study with similar findings, Bill Curtis presented a group of 60 professional programmers with what he characterized as a "simple" debugging task.[3] Curtis observed order of magnitude differences among the programmers who were able to complete the task.

More confirmation for the observation that personnel capabilities vary greatly comes from the Cocomo II estimation model.[4] The Cocomo II model uses numerous factors to adjust a base effort estimate. The effect of each factor has been calibrated using extensive statistical analysis of the Cocomo II project database. Seven of the Cocomo II model's 22 factors are related to personnel.

According to the Cocomo II model, the project team's applications-area experience exerts an influence on the project cost and effort of 1.51. In Cocomo-speak, that means that a project team with the least experience (bottom 15 percent) in an applications area will require 1.51 times as much effort to complete a project as the most experienced team (top 10 percent), all other factors being equal. The team's experience with the technical platform exerts an influence of 1.40, and experience with the programming language and tools exerts an influence of 1.43.

Requirements analyst capability (which refers to how good the analysts are, as opposed to how much experience they have) has an influence of 2.00. Programmer capability has an influence of 1.76. Communications factors (location of personnel and communication support such as e-mail, network, and so on) exert an influence of 1.53. Personnel continuity has an influence of 1.51.

These factors are summarized in Table 15-1.

The seniority-oriented factors alone (applications experience, language experience, and platform experience) exert an influence of 3.02. The seven personnel-oriented factors collectively exert a staggering influence range of 24.6! This simple fact accounts for much of the reason that nonprocess-oriented organizations such as Microsoft, Amazon.com, and other entrepreneurial powerhouses can experience industry-leading productivity while seemingly shortchanging process.

TABLE 15-1
Personnel influences in the Cocomo II estimation model

COCOMO II FACTOR	COCOMO II NAME	INFLUENCE
Applications experience	APEX	1.51
Communications factors	SITE	1.53
Language and tool experience	LTEX	1.43
Personnel continuity	PCON	1.51
Platform experience	PLEX	1.40
Programmer capability	PCAP	1.76
Analyst capability	ACAP	2.00
Cumulative		**24.6**

Low-Productivity Programmers

The range in productivity says that some programmers are much more productive than others, which implies that we'd like to find ways to hire and retain the best programmers. But that's only half the story. In DeMarco and Lister's study, 13 of the 166 programmers in the coding war games didn't finish the project *at all*—that's almost 10 percent of the programmers in the sample. In Curtis's study, 6 of the 60 professional programmers weren't able to complete the "simple" debugging task, again 10 percent.

What are the real-world implications of working with programmers who can't complete their work? In the studies mentioned, the results from programmers who didn't finish their assignments were excluded from the results of the study. On a real project, "excluding results" usually isn't an option, and so those programmers who can't finish would require either huge amounts of time to complete their work or someone else would have to complete their work for them. On real projects, these 10 to 1 differences in productivity might well translate into *productivity vs. anti-productivity*— eventually someone else will have to redo the work of programmers who can't finish their assignments. In other words, having the lowest-productivity programmers work on a project actually moves it backwards.

Low productivity in itself isn't the only problem. Strained to the limits of their abilities by the coding activity itself, low productivity programmers are either not able or not willing to follow project coding conventions or design standards. They don't remove most or all of the defects from their code before they integrate it with other people's work, or before other people are affected by it. They can't estimate their work reliably because they don't know for sure whether they will even finish. Considering the absence of direct contributions to the project and the extra work created for the rest of the team, it's no exaggeration to classify these programmers as "negative productivity programmers." The study data suggests that about 10 percent of professional programmers might fall into this category. A team of seven randomly selected programmers therefore has about a 50/50 chance of including at least one negative productivity programmer.

Physical Environment

Another finding from DeMarco and Lister's war games was that the developers whose productivity was in the top 25 percent had bigger, quieter, more private offices and fewer interruptions from people and phone calls than the other 75 percent. The differences in physical space weren't all that dramatic. The top 25 percent performers had an average of 78 square feet of dedicated floor space; the bottom 25 percent had 46 square feet.

The differences in productivity were more dramatic. Developers in the top quartile had productivity 2.6 times better than developers in the bottom 25 percent. In Cocomo II terms, the influence of office environment between the top tier (top quartile) and bottom tier (bottom quartile) is 2.6.

Motivation

Motivation is usually thought to be the greatest influence on how well people perform, and most productivity studies have found that motivation has a stronger influence on productivity than any other factor.[5]

Whatever else its critics might say about Microsoft, everyone agrees that it has succeeded in motivating its developers to an extraordinary degree. Stories of 12-, 14-, even 18-hour days are common, as are stories of people who live in their offices for weeks at a time. I know of one developer who had a Murphy bed custom-made to fit his office. In its local area, Microsoft is known as "The Velvet Sweatshop," which suggests that, if anything, Microsoft might be doing too good a job of motivating its employees.

Microsoft's approach to achieving this high level of motivation is simple. It explicitly focuses on morale. Each group at Microsoft has a morale budget that can be used for anything the group wants to use it for. Some groups buy movie-theater style popcorn poppers. Some groups go skiing or go bowling or have a cookout. Some groups make T-shirts. Some groups rent a whole movie theater for a private screening of their favorite movie.

Microsoft also makes extensive use of nonmonetary rewards. During the year I spent working at Microsoft, I received three team T-shirts, a team rugby shirt, a team beach towel, and a team mouse pad. I also took part in a team train ride and a nice dinner on the local "Dinner Train" and another dinner at a nice restaurant. If I had been a permanent employee, I would also have received a few more shirts, a Microsoft watch, a plaque for participating in the project, and a big Lucite "Ship-It" award for shipping the project. The total value of this stuff is only a few hundred dollars, but the psychological value is much greater.

Microsoft doesn't ignore developers' personal lives, either. During the time I was there, the developer who had the office next to mine had his 10-year-old daughter come by every day after school. She did her homework quietly in his office while he worked. No one at the company even raised an eyebrow.

In addition to providing explicit support for morale, Microsoft gladly trades other factors to keep morale high, sometimes trading them in ways that would make other companies shudder. I've seen them trade methodological purity, programming discipline, control over the product specification, control over the schedule, management visibility—almost anything to benefit morale. Regardless of the other effects, the motivational efficacy of this approach speaks for itself.

Staff Seniority

Falling in line with Cocomo's emphasis on staff seniority, many leading organizations recognize the importance of senior staff. Many years ago, the Director of Development at Microsoft pointed out to me that he had identified senior personnel as a critical success factor. He said that one of the keys to success of a product such as Microsoft Excel was to have at least two of the senior staff continue over from the previous release of the same product.

In a study of runaway projects in the United Kingdom, project managers identified "insufficient senior staff" as a contributing cause of project difficulties in approximately 40 percent of the projects that overran their schedules or budgets to a significant degree.[6]

Even organizations that focus strongly on software processes recognize the important role of human factors. The NASA Software Engineering Laboratory was the first organization to win the IEEE Computer Society's award for software process achievement. In their *Recommended Approach to Software Development, Revision 3* one of their top nine recommendations is "Do start the project with a small, senior staff."[7]

Bottom Line

It turns out that concentrating on technical expertise, staff continuity, business domain experience, private offices, motivation, and other human-oriented factors is a sound economic focus. The software industry needs an effective approach to software professionalism that will help identify the top tier performers, weed out the bottom tier performers, and raise the performance of the middle performers closer to the level of the best.

Notes

1. Sackman, H., W. J. Erikson, and E. E. Grant, "Exploratory Experimental Studies Comparing Online and Offline Programming Performance," *Communications of the ACM,* vol. 11, no. 1, January 1968, pp. 3–11.

2. DeMarco, Tom, and Timothy Lister, "Programmer Performance and the Effects of the Workplace," in *Proceedings of the 8th International Conference on Software Engineering,* August 1985.

3. Curtis, Bill, "Substantiating Programmer Variability," *Proceedings of the IEEE,* vol. 69, no. 7, 1981.

4. Boehm, Barry, et al., *Software Cost Estimation with Cocomo II,* Boston, MA: Addison-Wesley, 2000.

5. Boehm, Barry W., *Software Engineering Economics,* Englewood Cliffs, NJ: Prentice-Hall, Inc., 1981.

6. Cole, Andy, "Runaway Projects—Cause and Effects," *Software World,* vol. 26, no. 3, pp. 3–5.

7. NASA, *Recommended Approach to Software Development, Revision 3,* document number SEL-81-305, Greenbelt, MD: Goddard Space Flight Center, NASA, 1992.

CHAPTER SIXTEEN

Construx's Professional Development Program

How does a company support development of true software professionals? As I discussed in Chapter 6, overall software industry support for career development of software professionals is emerging, but still weak. Few universities offer undergraduate education in software engineering, and the number of graduates has fallen far short of the number needed to meet industry demands. This situation is improving rapidly, but it will still be years before university output is sufficient to meet industry needs.

Private industry is not supporting effective career development either. Rather than experiencing a career *progression,* most software workers simply move from one project to the next without any structured improvement of their skills. Few technology companies even try to offer career support for their software workers, and the software industry at large has nothing comparable to the career progression a physician would receive in a medical practice, an attorney would receive in a law practice, or an accountant would receive in an accounting practice.

This chapter is adapted from the Construx Software white paper "Construx's Professional Development Program," © 2002 Construx Software Builders, Inc. Used with permission. The current white paper can be downloaded from www.construx.com/profession. I am indebted to Jenny Stuart, who drafted the original white paper.

Because of my long-standing interest in software professionalism, several years ago I set out to create explicit career pathing and professional development support for the software engineers at my company, Construx Software. We identified specific objectives in creating a professional development program for our software engineers:

- *Skills enhancement.* The primary purpose of our professional development program is to improve the skills of our employees.
- *Career pathing.* Our program needed to provide a structured path for improving the capabilities of Construx's software engineers throughout their employment with Construx.
- *Support for common software job titles.* Our professional development program needed to support the full range of software job titles including software developers, testers, business analysts, project managers, architects, and other common industry positions.
- *Consistency.* For ease of administration, the professional development program needed to support consistent means of evaluating employee performance and promoting technical staff regardless of technical specialization.
- *Generalizability beyond Construx.* After implementing the professional development program within Construx, we wanted to be able to offer the program to other companies to support the career development of their software professionals.

Construx Knowledge Areas

The core of our professional development program is a Professional Development Ladder (PDL), which is based upon the SWEBOK knowledge areas described in Chapter 5. We call these knowledge areas Construx Knowledge Areas (CKAs). The CKAs define the body of knowledge that technical employees should understand and be able to apply. As described in Chapter 5, there are ten knowledge areas:

- Software Requirements
- Software Design
- Software Construction
- Software Testing
- Software Maintenance
- Software Configuration Management
- Software Quality
- Software Engineering Management
- Software Engineering Tools and Methods
- Software Engineering Process

Although the SWEBOK defines each of these knowledge areas in detail, we found that we needed to define specific interpretations of each knowledge area for our own use. Our specific interpretations are described in Table 16-1.

TABLE 16-1
Description of Construx Knowledge Areas (CKAs)

CKA	DESCRIPTION
Requirements	The discovery, analysis, modeling, and documentation of the functions to be implemented in software.
Design	The bridge between Requirements and Construction, Design defines the structure and dynamic state of the system at many levels of abstraction and through many views.
Construction	The creation of software according to a specified design. The primary activity is creating code and configuration data to implement functionality using the selected languages, technologies, and environments.
Testing	Activities associated with executing software to detect defects and evaluate features.
Maintenance	Activities related to system installation, deployment, migration, and operation.

continued

TABLE 16-1 *continued*

CKA	DESCRIPTION
Configuration Management	The discipline of defining how project artifacts are organized and stored, how changes to those artifacts are controlled and managed, and how the system is released to the customer.
Quality	Activities performed on static artifacts associated with providing confidence that a software item conforms or will conform to technical requirements.
Engineering Management	All aspects of management ranging from business and personnel management issues to project management issues.
Engineering Tools and Methods	The use of tools, technology, methodologies, and techniques for software engineering.
Process	Activities related to measuring and improving software development quality, timeliness, efficiency, productivity, and other project and product characteristics.

Capability Levels

The CKAs provide a tidy way of organizing software engineering knowledge, but they are not quite sufficient to identify a software engineer's capabilities. Consequently, within each CKA Construx recognizes four levels of *capability*: Introductory, Competency, Leadership, and Mastery. These capability levels support an engineer's progression of knowledge and experience within each knowledge area. Each CKA outlines the specific activities—such as reading, classes, and work experience—necessary to obtain each level of capability. Table 16-2 summarizes each of the capability levels.

We have found that capability depends on a combination of experience and knowledge. A person cannot truly possess leading-edge knowledge in an engineering discipline unless the knowledge is grounded in experience. Leading-edge experience is not possible unless it's fully apprised of state-of-the-art knowledge. Consequently, when there is a discrepancy between the levels of an employee's experience and knowledge, the overall capability of the employee is generally closer to the lesser of that employee's knowledge or experience. Figure 16-1 summarizes this concept.

TABLE 16-2
Summary of capability levels

CAPABILITY LEVEL	SUMMARY
Introductory	The employee performs basic work in an area, generally under supervision. The employee is taking effective steps to develop his or her knowledge and skills.
Competency	The employee performs effective, independent work in an area, serves as a role model for less expert employees, and occasionally coaches others.
Leadership	The employee performs exemplary work in an area. The employee regularly coaches employees and provides project-level and possibly company-wide leadership. The employee is recognized within Construx as a major resource in the knowledge area.
Mastery	The employee performs reference work in an area and has deep experience across multiple projects. The employee has generally taught seminars or classes or has written papers or books that extend the body of knowledge. The employee provides industry-level leadership and is recognized outside Construx for expertise in the area.

Knowledge \ Experience	Introductory	Competency	Leadership	Mastery
Introductory	Introductory	Competency	Competency	—
Competency	Competency	Competency	Competency	—
Leadership	Competency	Competency	Leadership	Mastery
Mastery	—	—	Mastery	Mastery

FIGURE 16-1
Overall capability as a function of knowledge and experience.

Professional Development Ladder Levels

Combining knowledge areas and capability levels allows us to build career ladder levels. Ladder levels provide the mechanism for advancement and promotion. Moving up the ladder requires an engineer to obtain both additional breadth (more knowledge areas) and depth (improved capability within knowledge areas). It requires an increase in both knowledge and experience.

For historical reasons, our ladder levels go from 9 to 15. College graduates will generally start at Level 9, while experienced engineers may start at Level 10 or 11. Level 12 is considered full professional status at Construx. Many engineers within Construx choose not to go beyond Level 12, as Levels 13 to 15 can only be achieved by making significant, innovative contributions both to Construx and to the field of software engineering.

Table 16-3 describes each of the ladder levels and outlines the requirements for entering each level.

TABLE 16-3

Professional Development Ladder level requirements

LADDER LEVEL	DESCRIPTION	CKAS COVERED
9	A Level 9 engineer is beginning to learn the principles of software engineering and is generally just out of school. This person works under close supervision.	Not applicable.
10	A Level 10 engineer has some background in software engineering. This person either is recently out of school or has 1 to 2 years work experience. He or she is capable of performing work with limited supervision.	Introductory in all CKAs. Competence in 3 CKAs.
11	A Level 11 engineer has a fairly strong background in software engineering and can work independently as necessary. This person has worked on one or more completed projects and has experience in each of the basic software development lifecycle steps needed to release a product.	Introductory in all CKAs. Competence in 6 CKAs. Leadership in 1 CKA.

TABLE 16-3 *continued*

LADDER LEVEL	DESCRIPTION	CKAS COVERED
12	A Level 12 engineer has consistently had "wins" during his or her participation in all aspects of small and large projects and has been essential to those projects' successes. This person has a track record of consistently rendering clear technical judgment and routinely considering project-level issues. A Level 12 engineer is innovative, consistent, and contributes beyond the assigned tasks. He or she generally provides technical guidance to or supervises others.	Introductory in all CKAs. Competence in 8 CKAs. Leadership in 3 CKAs.
13	A Level 13 engineer is a champion who can consider both internal and external aspects of a project and ensure they are handled correctly and with consistently sound judgment. This person takes total ownership for all aspects of his or her project and makes many unique contributions. This engineer's decisions have a significant impact on Construx's profitability and overall well-being.	Introductory in all CKAs. Competence in 8 CKAs. Leadership in 5 CKAs. Mastery in 1 CKA.
14	A Level 14 engineer is a major technical resource to others in the company. This person consistently overcomes very difficult technical challenges, and makes key decisions on the goals and structure of Construx. A Level 14 engineer is familiar to many working software engineers both inside and outside Construx for one or more specific contributions that have advanced the art and science of software engineering. This person's areas of capability extend beyond company-level issues to industry-level issues. Work at this level requires a career-long commitment to the field of software engineering, including significant work outside of the Construx workday.	Intentionally not defined.
15	A Level 15 engineer is indispensable to Construx's success. This person consistently works to design and produce groundbreaking, world-class products.	Intentionally not defined.

continued

TABLE 16-3 *continued*

LADDER LEVEL	DESCRIPTION	CKAS COVERED
	Working software engineers both within and outside Construx regard this person as a leader within the software engineering field. He or she takes primary responsibility for defining corporate practices. This person contributes frequently to the industry in numerous and varied ways. Work at this level requires a career-long commitment to the field of software engineering, including significant work outside of the Construx workday, and requires a degree of industry recognition for accomplishments that is well beyond the person's direct control.	

Ladder-Based Career Progression

To illustrate how Construx's Professional Development Ladder supports career development, consider the progression of a technically oriented engineer from Level 10 to Level 12. The target leadership areas for this engineer are Engineering Tools and Methods, Design, and Construction.

Figure 16-2 shows the requirements for the engineer to reach Level 10. For each level, the boxes indicate the obtained capability level in each CKA.

As Figure 16-3 illustrates, to reach Level 11, the engineer adds depth by achieving Leadership in Construction and breadth by obtaining Competency in several other CKAs.

As Figure 16-4 shows, to reach Level 12, the engineer achieves Leadership in Design and Engineering Tools and Methods and obtains Competency in two additional CKAs.

The Professional Development Ladder supports a variety of career paths by allowing technical staff members to select the knowledge areas they wish to focus on. This provides both flexibility and structure as each person may guide his or her specific career path within the constraints of the capability level/CKA requirements. In the example shown in Figures

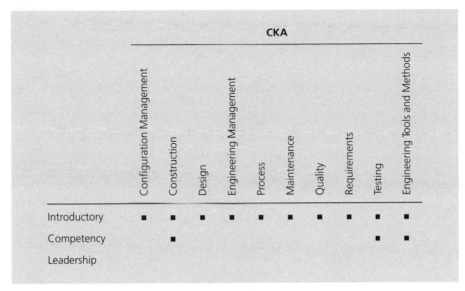

FIGURE 16-2
Sample Professional Development Ladder requirements to reach Level 10.

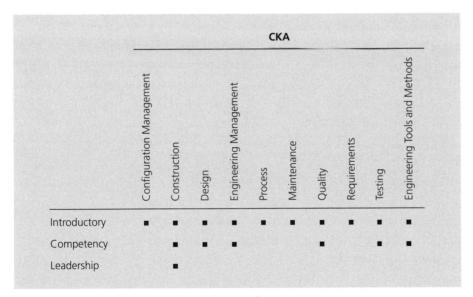

FIGURE 16-3
Sample Professional Development Ladder requirements to reach Level 11.

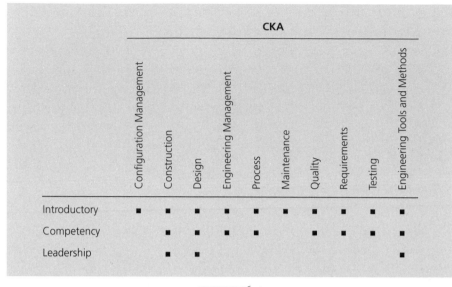

FIGURE 16-4

Sample Professional Development Ladder requirements to reach Level 12.

16-2 through 16-4, the developer has focused on Engineering Tools and Methods, Design, and Construction. In other cases, an engineer with a management orientation might focus on Engineering Management, Process, and Requirements. An engineer with a quality orientation might focus on Quality, Process, and Testing. Construx's Professional Development Ladder provides a consistent means of defining career progression regardless of the engineer's orientation.

CKA Requirements at Different Capability Levels

The ladder contains four capability levels, but the Mastery level is not describable in advance (by definition), so we typically refer to our Ladder as a 10×3 matrix of 10 CKAs and 3 capability levels—for a total of 30 unique capability areas. Within each capability area of the capability level/ CKA matrix there is a set of specific activities, such as reading, classes, and work experience, which must be completed to meet that capability area's requirements. In total, the Professional Development Ladder is comprised of nearly 1,000 specific requirements at this time.

The Engineering Management CKA provides a good example of the extent of the requirements for the Introductory, Competency, and Leadership capability levels. Table 16-4 shows the reading and work experience necessary to achieve Introductory capability in Engineering Management.

As Table 16-5 illustrates, significantly more effort is required to achieve Competency capability in the Engineering Management area.

Moving from Competency to Leadership in a CKA is not as predetermined as moving from Introductory to Competency. Detailed requirements are defined jointly between the employee, the employee's mentor, and the employee's manager. At the Leadership level, in addition to reading, classes, and work experience, the employee may also be required to

TABLE 16-4

Introductory level requirements in Engineering Management

TYPE OF ACTIVITY	REQUIREMENTS
Reading	The following materials must be read *analytically*:[1] • "They Write the Right Stuff," Charles Fishman[2] • *Software Project Survival Guide,* Steve McConnell[3] • "Software Engineering Code of Ethics and Professionalism," ACM/IEEE-CS[4] The following materials must be read *inspectionally*: • *201 Principles of Software Development,* Alan Davis[5] • *Software Engineering,* Part 1 + Chapters 22 & 23, Ian Sommerville[6] • *Software Engineering: A Practitioner's Approach,* Chapter 4, Roger Pressman[7]
Work Experience	• Review a project plan • Learn an estimation technique • Plan and track personal activities
Classes	None
Certifications	None
Industry Participation	None

TABLE 16-5
Competency level requirements in Engineering Management

TYPE OF ACTIVITY	REQUIREMENTS
Reading	The following materials must be read *analytically*: • "No Silver Bullets—Essence and Accidents of Software Engineering," Fred Brooks[8] • "Programmer Performance and the Effects of the Workplace," DeMarco and Lister[9] • "Manager's Handbook for Software Development," NASA Goddard Space Flight Center[10] • *Rapid Development,* Steve McConnell[11] The following materials must be read *inspectionally*: • "Software's Chronic Crisis," Wayt Gibbs[12] • "Recommended Approach to Software Development," NASA Goddard Space Flight Center[13]
Work Experience	• Participate as a reviewer for a project's management artifacts • Participate in the creation of a project charter • Participate in the creation of a project plan • Participate in the creation of a project estimate; become proficient with individual bottom-up estimation techniques; lead an estimation activity • Become proficient with individual status reporting techniques; create a weekly status report • Become proficient with work planning (including work breakdown structures, estimation, and earned value management)
Classes	• Software Project Survival Guide (2 days) • Rapid Development (2 days) • Software Estimation (2 days)
Certifications	None
Industry Participation	None

obtain recognized industry certifications and to participate at the industry level by teaching classes, giving conference presentations, and so on.

Table 16-6 details the kinds of activities and level of effort required for this transition.

TABLE 16-6

Example of Leadership level requirements in Engineering Management

TYPE OF ACTIVITY	REQUIREMENTS
Reading	Reading is customized at the Leadership level. The focus area and selection of specific books and articles are worked out with the mentor and outlined in the Professional Development Plan. A rough target of about 1,000 pages is required to move from Competency to Leadership in each CKA.
Work Experience	• Lead planning, estimation, and tracking activities for a significant project; create a project charter with business case; create a project plan for a large and a small project; create a work plan for a significant project; proficient with lifecycle selection, customization, and planning; proficient with formal risk management techniques; proficient with formal issue management techniques; lead issue management for a significant project; proficient with historical data collection techniques. • Proficient in-group estimation techniques (e.g., wide-band Delphi), analogy estimation techniques, and parametric estimation techniques; create a top-down project estimate at project inception. • Create a business (or milestone) schedule for a significant project; create a detailed schedule for a milestone; proficient with critical-path and critical-chain scheduling techniques (Gantt and PERT); proficient with project status reporting techniques. • Participate in consulting/coaching work in engineering management.
Classes	• Effective Software Project Management (3 days) • Risk Management (2 days) • Project Outsourcing (2 days)
Certifications	• Obtain IEEE Computer Society's Certified Software Development Professional certification.[14] • Obtain PMI's Project Management Professional certification.[15]
Industry Participation	At the Leadership level, employees are expected to contribute significantly within Construx and potentially to the industry at large. Examples of the industry participation expected at this level include: • Create evening, weekend, or college course in this area; teach an evening, weekend, or college class.

continued

TABLE 16-6 *continued*

TYPE OF ACTIVITY	REQUIREMENTS
	• Teach a Construx seminar or university course. • Participate in an industry committee, panel, group, standards board, etc. • Present at a conference. • Publish an article in major or peer-reviewed publication. • Publish an article in a second-tier publication. • Review a book manuscript. • Review articles for *IEEE Software* or similar publication. • Actively mentor and coach other Construx employees in the leadership area.

Lessons Learned from the Professional Development Ladder

Version 1.0 of the Professional Development Ladder was deployed within Construx in 1998 and released to the public shortly thereafter. Since then, we have continued to evolve the ladder, releasing Version 2.0 internally in early 2002. During this time, we learned a number of important lessons about deploying and supporting a Professional Development Ladder.

Structural and Cultural Reinforcements

To successfully support an organization's professional development, the Professional Development Ladder must become engrained in the culture of the organization. We have found that numerous reinforcements are needed to ensure employee buy-in and achieve the desired benefits.

While adoption of the specific reinforcements used at Construx is not essential to successful deployment of a Professional Development Ladder, it is important to identify structural and cultural reinforcements that will work within any particular organization.

Construx's specific structural and cultural reinforcements include the following programs.

Professional Development Plans. Professional Development Plans (PDPs) provide a mechanism to plan, track, and document an employee's progression along the ladder. Each PDP outlines the short- and long-term goals of the employee and describes the specific activities (reading, classes, work experience, and other professional activities) that will occur between the current and next review cycle.

The goals of a PDP virtually always include a grade level promotion within a one to five year horizon. The plan outlines the work an engineer needs to accomplish in that timeframe to achieve the promotion. Further than one year out, the final details of the work are not fully described, but a high-level path is outlined. When an engineer is within one year of a promotion, the details of the work are described month-by-month to manager, mentor, and employee. The PDPs support objective and consistent promotion criteria throughout Construx.

Mentoring Program. Mentors provide guidance and support as an engineer progresses up the Professional Development Ladder. All technical employees at Construx develop and discuss their PDPs with their mentors. Mentoring allows tailoring of the Professional Development Ladder to provide relevant and practical professional development plans for each employee. To ensure that knowledge requirements are met by the employee, employees and mentors meet about six to eight times a year; more often when the employee is within six months of a grade level promotion.

Active manager and mentor interaction is critical to ensure the progress and completion of activities in the PDP. To support this, the division Vice President and mentor must both sign the employee's PDP. Additionally, mentor meetings track the employee's progress against the plan and, if appropriate, adjust expectations about the timing of a promotion.

One of the goals of the mentor program is to produce professional engineers dedicated and self-directed in further professional development. Engineers at Level 12 and above are expected to be self-directed, and so they do not have mentors unless they specifically request a mentor or wish to work toward an additional grade level promotion.

Professional Development Plaques. Construx recognizes numerous significant milestones that occur during an employee's professional development—grade-level promotions, achievement of professional certifications, first leadership roles on projects, first classes taught, first papers published, and other significant accomplishments. Each technical employee receives a Professional Development Plaque that contains engraved plates commemorating significant accomplishments. These plaques provide a way to commemorate important milestones and reflect the importance Construx places on ongoing professional development.

Training Program. Construx targets 10 to 12 days of focused training per work year in addition to the on-the-job training that occurs inherently in software development work. At lower experience levels, focused training consists mainly of attending classes and conferences. At Level 12 and above, training can consist of preparing for conference presentations, participating in standards committees, organizing special interest groups, and other professional activities.

Salary Structure. We've found that an organization's traditional reward system must be structured to support professional development goals; otherwise, project goals will supercede development goals. By basing promotions, salaries, and performance reviews on the ladder, the emphasis on professional development is firmly engrained in the organization.

Our ladder levels have exactly one salary level at each level. The salary for each ladder level and each employee's ladder level is public information within Construx. Employees have a tangible incentive to reach the next ladder level because they know the salary adjustment that will occur with that promotion.

Software Engineering Discussion Groups. Software Engineering Discussion Groups (SEDGs) provide a forum to gain and share software engineering knowledge. They are moderated forums in which a book from the Professional Development Ladder is discussed and debated. Levels 9, 10, and 11 have an SEDG. Level 12 engineers are encouraged to join the SEDGs as a way of sharing experience and knowledge with more junior engineers.

Level 12 Recognition. Attaining Level 12—full professional status at Construx—represents a significant achievement in a software engineer's career at Construx. In recognition of this achievement, Construx provides a bonus equal to one year's difference in salary from Level 11 to Level 12, a reception in honor of the promotion, an advertisement in a local business newspaper, and a portrait in our lobby. This recognition symbolizes the importance we place on professional development.

Assimilating Experienced Engineers into the Ladder

We found a need to accommodate new employees who gained their experience at other companies. Many of our job candidates have had extensive industry experience but have not met some of our other ladder requirements. Hiring these employees at our Level 10 or Level 11 salaries would make our offers noncompetitive. As a practical matter, we wouldn't be able to hire many senior engineers. It became important to determine how a new employee could be brought in at Level 12 without compromising the integrity of the ladder and without diminishing the achievements of Construx employees who have worked their way up the ladder while at Construx.

To support these goals, we created "Transitional Level 12." A Transitional Level 12 Engineer is hired as a Level 12 Engineer and has one year or less to complete the missing elements of the ladder, typically extensive reading. During this year, the employee meets with a mentor monthly to discuss the work he or she has completed and to deal with any progress issues. When backfilling is complete, the employee is recognized as a Level 12 Engineer.

Benefits of the Professional Development Ladder

After five years of using Version 1 and Version 2 of our PDL, we have realized numerous benefits.

- *Accelerated professional development.* We have achieved our primary goal of improving the skills of our technical employees, and development occurs surprisingly quickly. When interviewing candidates for technical jobs, we typically find that our internal standards for a Construx engineer with two or three years of experience are comparable to many companies' standards for their most senior engineers.

- *Team capability.* By standardizing on the CKAs, our staff has developed a shared knowledge and experience base. This has improved communication among our staff and supports highly efficient specialized leadership roles.

- *Well-liked promotion criteria.* We've found that our technical staff appreciates the openness of our promotion structure. They feel that they can be in control of their own career development, and they feel that they actually have careers, not just jobs.

- *Hiring.* Basing our internal work on the CKAs provides us with a straightforward way to assess technical job candidates. We can assess candidates according to their capabilities in each CKA. We have found that assessment of candidates by different members of our staff is remarkably consistent.

- *Anti-hiring.* Our ladder requires a level of personal accountability that some prospective employees do not like. Making our professional development expectations explicit during the hiring process allows us to weed out candidates who are not serious about software engineering.

- *Skills inventory management.* The 10×3 CKA matrix gives us a natural, structured way of tracking the capabilities of our company's software engineering staff.

- *Morale and retention.* Although the Professional Development Ladder is only one piece of the equation, we believe it substantially contributes to our company's high retention and morale. At the time I am writing this, Construx has been a finalist in *Washington CEO Magazine's* Best Small Companies to Work For competition three years in a row, and we have not lost a technical employee to voluntary turnover in more than three years.

Using the Ladder Outside Construx

Construx has used the Professional Development Ladder to provide structured and flexible support for career development within Construx. By defining and developing capabilities across numerous CKAs, Construx ensures that our staff has both depth and breadth—which is consistent with an engineering approach to software development. Through the flexible ladder framework, our technical staff can choose career progressions well matched to their interests.

Construx's capability requirements are more intensive than most companies' requirements due to our corporate mission of "Advancing the Art and Science of Commercial Software Engineering." Most of our senior software engineers consult, teach, and lead projects, which means more of our employees need to achieve Leadership levels than employees in other organizations.

We have found that basing the ladder on the SWEBOK knowledge areas has provided us with significant advantages. Factoring the CKAs into a 10×3 matrix means that the Professional Development Ladder can easily be tailored to add or remove capability levels, knowledge areas, and specific ladder requirements for the needs of other software organizations. Using the 10×3 structure, specific career paths—for example, Project Manager, Business Analyst, Developer, and Tester—can be defined on top of the Professional Development Ladder to provide structure and guidance within an organization that doesn't wish to expose the inner workings of the ladder to its staff.

The details will vary when the ladder is deployed within different organizations, but the ladder's structure and key concepts can be deployed in any organization. The underlying ladder foundation provides a high degree of integrity in each case.

Notes

1. Construx's ladder differentiates between "analytical" and "inspectional" reading levels. For details on this distinction, see Steve McConnell, "How to Read a Technical Article," *IEEE Software,* Nov./Dec. 1998, pp. 128f.

2. Fishman, Charles, "They Write the Right Stuff," *Fast Company,* December 1996.

3. McConnell, Steve, *Software Project Survival Guide,* Redmond, WA: Microsoft Press, 1998.

4. See www.construx.com/profession.

5. Davis, Alan M., *201 Principles of Software Development,* New York: McGraw-Hill, 1995.

6. Sommerville, Ian, *Software Engineering,* 6th Ed., Boston, MA: Addison-Wesley, 2000.

7. Pressman, Roger S., *Software Engineering: A Practitioner's Approach,* 5th Ed., New York: McGraw-Hill, 2001.

8. Brooks, Frederick P., Jr., "No Silver Bullets—Essence and Accidents of Software Engineering," *Computer,* April 1987, pp. 10–19.

9. DeMarco, Tom, and Timothy Lister, "Programmer Performance and the Effects of the Workplace," *Proceedings of the 8th International Conference on Software Engineering,* August 1985, pp. 268–272.

10. *Manager's Handbook for Software Development, Revision 1,* Document number SEL-84-101, Greenbelt, MD: Goddard Space Flight Center, NASA, 1990.

11. McConnell, Steve, *Rapid Development.* Redmond, WA: Microsoft Press, 1996.

12. Gibbs, W. Wayt, "Software's Chronic Crisis," *Scientific American,* September 1994, pp. 86–95.

13. *Recommended Approach to Software Development, Revision 3,* Document number SEL-81-305, Greenbelt, MD: Goddard Space Flight Center, NASA, 1992.

14. See www.computer.org/certification.

15. See www.pmi.org.

PART FOUR

Industry Professionalism

CHAPTER SEVENTEEN

Engineering a Profession

Engineering can provide a life of genuine satisfaction in many ways, especially through ministering in a practical manner to the needs and welfare of mankind.

VANNEVAR BUSH

Engineers are saddled with much the same stereotype as computer programmers. They are regarded as boring and dull, and yet these boring and dull engineers are responsible for some of the most exciting developments in the world today. Putting a man on the moon, viewing the outer reaches of space from the Hubble Space Telescope, flying on modern jet aircraft, driving coast to coast in cars that operate nearly flawlessly, connecting to Internet sites throughout the world, enjoying theater-quality video presentations at home—these technological miracles are all predominately engineering accomplishments, the practical application of scientific principles.

Need for Engineering

Historically, professional engineering has been established in response to threats to public safety. Although we take the safety of modern bridges for granted, in the 1860s American bridges were failing at the rate of 25 or more per year.[1] Bridge failures and the loss of life they caused precipitated creation of a stricter engineering approach to bridge design and construction. In Canada, engineering folklore holds that the collapse of the Quebec City bridge in 1907 catalyzed establishment of higher standards in all branches of Canadian engineering, which is symbolized today in the iron ring ceremony.[2] (I'll describe that ceremony in more detail in Chapter 19.) Engineers in Texas were licensed only after a boiler explosion in an elementary school killed more than 300 children in 1937.[3] The part that caused the explosion in 1937 has been replaced today by software.

Engineering differs from other professions in that doctors, dentists, public accountants, and lawyers generally provide their services to specific individuals or, in some cases, to specific corporations. Engineers tend to design *things* rather than provide services to individuals. Their responsibility is more often to society than to specific people. In this sense, software developers are more like engineers than they are like other kinds of professionals.

Software hasn't yet had its Quebec City bridge or its Texas elementary school boiler. But the potential is real. As any reader of the Forum on Risks to the Public in the Use of Computers and Related Systems[4] knows, software has already been responsible for many multi-million dollar losses, ranging from the ridiculous to the deadly. Tsutomu Shimomura parked on February 29, 1992, at a San Diego airport parking lot. When he returned six days later, his parking bill was $3,771. The parking software didn't recognize February 29 as a valid date.[5] In January 1990, approximately five million telephone calls were blocked over a nine-hour period because of a software error. The first space shuttle launch was delayed for two days because of a subtle programming error. The Mariner I space probe to Venus was lost because of an error in transcribing a guidance equation into software. In London, a computer dispatch system for ambulances was placed into operation before it was ready, collapsed completely, and caused delays as long as 11 hours. As many as 20 deaths were attributed to the new ambulance dispatch system. Iran Air Flight 655 was shot down by the USS *Vincennes*'s Aegis system in 1988, killing 290 people. The error was initially attributed to operator error, but later some experts attributed the incident to the poor design of Aegis's user interface.

Engineering and Art

Engineering's use of mathematics and science exposes it to the criticism that it is dry—that it saps the artistic elements out of structures that are engineered. The same criticism has been applied to software engineering. How true is this criticism? Does engineering exclude aesthetics?

Far from being antithetical to aesthetics, engineering is largely concerned with all aspects of design, including aesthetic aspects. Its designs aren't just limited to shapes and colors. Engineers design everything from electronic circuits to load-bearing beams to vehicles that land on the moon. As Samuel C. Florman says in *The Existential Pleasures of Engineering,* "Creative design is the central mission of the professional engineer."

Consider a comparison of two well-known buildings, the Reims Cathedral and the Sydney Opera House. The Reims Cathedral, shown in Figure 17-1, was completed about 1290; the Sydney Opera House, shown in Figure 17-2, in 1973. The Reims Cathedral was designed to use materials whose properties were understood (more or less) at the time.

The Sydney Opera House was constructed 700 years after the Reims Cathedral. As you can see in Figure 17-2, it's stylistically quite different from the Reims Cathedral. Its architects used modern materials such as steel and reinforced concrete, and they employed engineering techniques including computer modeling to determine how little material could safely be used.

Which building you prefer is a matter of taste, but which building can actually be built is a matter of engineering. It would be possible for modern builders to construct another Reims Cathedral, but it would not have been possible for 13th century builders to construct a Sydney Opera House. The reason the Sydney Opera House could not be built in the 13th century was not a lack of art, but the lack of engineering. We've all seen ugly buildings in which artistic considerations lost a battle with engineering economy, or in which aesthetics appear not to have been considered at all. Engineering without art can be ugly, but art without engineering may be impossible. Engineering does not constrain artistic possibilities. The *lack* of engineering constrains artistic possibilities.

FIGURE 17-1

Reims Cathedral, Reims, France. An example of art without very well developed engineering.[6]

FIGURE 17-2

Sydney Opera House, Sydney, Australia. An example of the dependence of art upon engineering.[7]

So it is with modern software systems. The level of engineering prowess determines how large a software system can be built successfully, how easy it will be to use, how fast it will operate, how many errors it will contain, and how well it will cooperate with other systems. Software includes many aesthetic elements, and software developers have no lack of artistic ambition. What we in the software industry sometimes lack is the engineering techniques that enable us to realize some of our grandest aesthetic aspirations.

Maturation of Engineering Disciplines

Disasters in older engineering fields have precipitated the professionalization of engineering practices in those fields. Of course, full-fledged engineering disciplines can't simply be willed into existence overnight. Mary Shaw at Carnegie Mellon University has identified a progression that fields go through before they reach the level of professional engineering. Figure 17-3 summarizes this maturation.

In the *craft* stage, good work is performed by talented amateurs. Craftsmen use intuition and brute force to create their widgets, whether their widgets are bridges, electric equipment, or computer programs. Some of their work is intended for sale to the public, but most is created solely for their own use. They have little or no concept of large-scale production

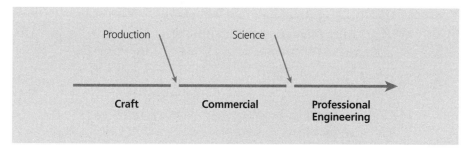

FIGURE 17-3
The progression of a discipline from craft to professional engineering.
Source: Adapted from "Prospects for an Engineering Discipline of Software"[8]

for external sale. Craftsmen tend to make extravagant use of available materials. The field progresses haphazardly; there's no systematic way to educate or train other craftsmen in the use of the most effective techniques.

Civil engineering (aqueduct and bridge construction) in first century Rome was a discipline in its craft stage, as was early computing in the 1950s and 1960s. Many software projects today still make extravagant use of available materials (staff time) and operate at the craft level.

At some point, the demand for the widgets increases beyond what isolated craftsmen can provide, and demand for greater production begins to influence the discipline. As the folklore becomes better understood, it's codified into written heuristics and procedural rules.

In the *commercial* stage, workers more carefully define the resources needed to support production. The stage is marked by a stronger economic orientation, and cost of goods may become an issue. Practitioners are trained to ensure consistent quality of the widgets they produce. Production procedures are systematically refined by changing different parameters to see what works and what doesn't.

The Reims Cathedral was built at a time when civil engineering was in its commercial stage. In software, many commercial-stage organizations achieve respectable levels of quality and productivity by making use of carefully selected, well-trained personnel. They rely on familiar practices and change them incrementally in pursuit of better products and better project performance.

Some of the problems encountered by commercial production can't be solved via trial and error, and, if the economic stakes are high enough, a corresponding science will develop. As the science matures, it develops theories that contribute to commercial practice, and this is the point at which the field reaches the *professional engineering* stage. At this point, progress arises from application of scientific principles as well as from practical experimentation. The practitioners working in the field at that point must be well-educated in both the theory and practice of their profession.

A Science for Software Development

Software science has been lagging behind commercial software development for years. Extremely large software systems were developed in the 1950s and 1960s, including the Sage missile defense system, the Sabre airline-reservation system, and IBM's OS/360 operating system. Commercial development of these large systems proceeded much faster than supporting research did, but practical applications advancing faster than science has been common in engineering. The airfoil wing section that allows airplanes to fly was invented just after it had been "proved" that no machine heavier than air could fly.[9] The development of thermodynamics followed the invention of the steam engine. When John Roebling designed the Brooklyn Bridge in the 1860s, the strength of steel cables was not well understood, and so he designed different parts of the bridge with safety margins as high as 6 to 1. This safety margin was an engineering judgment made in lieu of better theoretical knowledge.

The science that supports software development isn't as well defined as the physics that supports civil engineering. In fact it isn't even considered "natural science." It is what Herbert Simon calls a "science of the artificial"[10]—the knowledge areas of computer science, mathematics, psychology, sociology, and management science. A few software organizations regularly apply theories from these areas to their projects, but we are a long way from seeing universal application of these sciences of the artificial to software projects.

But are we really asking software science to provide the right things? For many classes of applications—inventory management systems, payroll programs, general ledger software, operating system design, database management software, language compilers (the list is nearly endless)—the same basic applications have been written so many times that these systems shouldn't require as much unique design effort as they seem to need. Mary Shaw points out that in mature engineering fields routine design involves solving familiar problems and reusing large portions of prior solutions. Often these "solutions" are codified in the form of equations, analytical models, or prebuilt components. Unique design challenges do present themselves from time to time, but the bread and butter of engineering is the application of routine design practices to familiar problems.

The software world is still in the process of capturing many of its "solutions" in ways that are useful to the average practitioner. Many software project artifacts are potentially reusable, and many of them promise more potential to improve quality and productivity than the most commonly reused artifact, source code, does. Here is a short list of some project artifacts that can be reused:[11]

- Architectures themselves and software design procedures
- Design patterns
- Requirements themselves and requirements engineering procedures
- User interface elements and user interface design procedures
- Estimates themselves and estimation procedures
- Planning data, project plans, and planning procedures
- Test plans, test cases, test data, and test procedures
- Technical review procedures
- Source code, construction procedures, and integration procedures
- Software configuration management procedures
- Post-project reports and project-review procedures
- Organizational structures, team structures, and management procedures

At present, few of these project artifacts have been packaged into a form that the average organization can readily apply.

Science has not yet provided software development with a set of equations that describe how to run a project successfully, or that describe how to produce successful software products. Perhaps it never will. But science doesn't necessarily have to consist of formulas and mathematics. In *The Structure of Scientific Revolutions,*[12] Thomas Kuhn points out that a scientific paradigm can consist of a set of solved problems. Reusable software project artifacts are a set of solved problems—solved requirements problems, design problems, planning problems, management problems, and so on.

The Call of Engineering

Arthur C. Clarke said that "any sufficiently advanced technology is indistinguishable from magic." Software technology is sufficiently advanced, and the general public is mystified by it. The public doesn't understand the safety risks posed by its software products or the financial risks posed by its software projects. As high priests of this powerful magic, software developers have a professional responsibility to use their magic wisely.

The engineering approach to design and construction has a track record of all but eliminating some of the most serious risks to public safety while supporting some of the most elevating expressions of the human spirit. Whether the goal is safety, aesthetics, or economics, treating software as an engineering discipline is an effective way to raise software development to the level of a true profession.

Notes

1. Florman, Samuel C., *The Existential Pleasures of Engineering,* 2d Ed., NY: St. Martin's Griffin, 1994.

2. I call this "folklore" because several Canadian professional engineers have independently told me that the iron in the iron ring traditionally is thought to come from the wreckage of the iron bridge that collapsed in Quebec City in 1907. Published information about the Canadian iron ring ceremony contains no mention of the Quebec City bridge. The ceremony itself might contain mention of this bridge, but it is a secret ceremony.

3. *The New York Times,* May 3, 1999.

4. Digest subscription to this forum is available by e-mailing risks-request@csl.sri.com or on Usenet at comp.risks.

5. All the examples in this paragraph come from Peter G. Neumann, *Computer-Related Risks,* Reading, MA: Addison-Wesley, 1995.

6. This image was obtained from IMSI's MasterClips©/MasterPhotos© collection, 1895 Francisco Blvd. East, San Rafael, CA 94901-5506, USA.

7. This image was obtained from IMSI's MasterClips©/MasterPhotos© collection, 1895 Francisco Blvd. East, San Rafael, CA 94901-5506, USA.

8. Shaw, Mary, "Prospects for an Engineering Discipline of Software," *IEEE Software,* November 1990, pp. 15f.

9. Christopher Alexander, quoted in Glass, Robert L., *Software Creativity,* Englewood Cliffs, NJ: Prentice Hall PTR, 1994.

10. Simon, Herbert, *The Sciences of the Artificial,* 3d Ed., Cambridge, MA: MIT Press, 1996.

11. For more information, see Jones, Capers, *Assessment and Control of Software Risks,* Englewood Cliffs, NJ: Yourdon Press, 1994.

12. Kuhn, Thomas S., *The Structure of Scientific Revolutions,* 3d Ed., Chicago: The University of Chicago Press, 1996.

CHAPTER EIGHTEEN

Hard Knocks

*Natural abilities are like natural plants, that need pruning
by study; and studies themselves do give forth directions too
much at large, except they be bounded in by experience.*

FRANCIS BACON

As I've hinted earlier, most software developers obtain their occupational education from the school of hard knocks. Experience can be a good teacher, but it is also a slow and expensive one.

A common lament among experienced software developers is that colleges don't teach students the skills they need to perform effectively on the job. An examination of current demographics in software developer education and training seems to bear this out. I argued in Chapter 4 that North American universities are providing computer-science rather than software-engineering educations. I left many of the implications of that distinction unexplored, and I would like to explore those implications here.

Industry has become less and less satisfied with university output. Capers Jones points out that, since the mid-1980s, large corporations in the United States have had more in-house instructors teaching software engineering topics than all universities combined.[1] Many of those corporations offer more comprehensive software engineering course catalogs than virtually any university catalog.

The Boeing Company studied the computer science curricula of more than 200 universities in the United States.[2] It wanted to identify programs that were producing graduates with the skills needed to perform satisfactorily at Boeing. It found that only about half the programs were accredited by the Computer Science Accreditation Board (CSAB)*, and only about half of the accredited programs were producing graduates that met Boeing's requirements. Some of the programs are more practically oriented, but they become more practical by teaching software engineering under the guise of computer science, which diffuses their focus on true computer science.

For engineering jobs, however, Boeing will accept applications from graduates of any program accredited by the Accreditation Board for Engineering and Technology (ABET). Boeing does not accept applications for engineering jobs from graduates of unaccredited schools. This suggests that computer science curriculum and accreditation standards are of questionable value to industry. A significant percentage of programs do not meet industry's needs. In contrast, the value of engineering curriculum and accreditation is so consistent that companies such as Boeing can hire from accredited engineering schools without doing any university-program screening themselves.

The questionable relevance of computer science education to industry provides one explanation for the decline and stagnation in undergraduate computer science degrees that students earned from 1985 through 1997. As Figure 18-1 shows, the number of undergraduate computer science degrees declined from a high of about 42,000 annually in 1985 to a low of about 24,000 in 1990 to 1997.

In recent years (1998 to 2000), we've seen a significant uptick in computer science students. I think both the decline and the uptick deserve examination.

The conventional explanation for the long decline was that students found computer science dull.[3] I don't find computer science dull, and I don't find the conventional wisdom persuasive. The real answer had been staring us in the face for many years: The number of students obtaining computer science degrees declined because education in computer science had become increasingly irrelevant to job-market requirements. Students

---

* At the time this observation was made, computer science programs were accredited by CSAB. Those programs are now accredited by ABET/CAC.

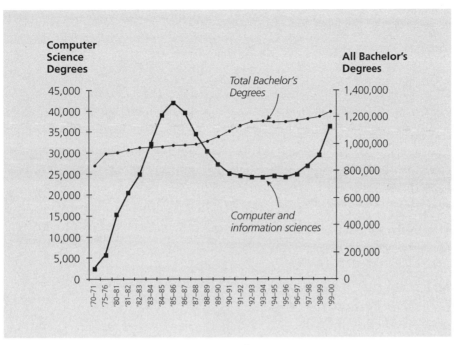

FIGURE 18-1

The number of undergraduate computer science degrees awarded has varied in recent years.

Source: National Center for Education Statistics[4]

knew they could get jobs without computer science degrees, and employers didn't universally value them. The old educational system wasn't working, and so it needed to be changed.

In the period from 1998 to 2000, two changes began to take place. First, the Internet caused a surge of excitement among undergraduate students. Gold Rush Fever kicked in, and more students began preparing for jobs in the software industry. Second, demands from the dot com economy of the late 1990s rippled into the university system, and universities began making computer science curriculums relevant again after several years of declining enrollments.

Development of Professional Engineers

As I've argued throughout the book, engineering makes a good model for a profession of software development, and the professional-development path that engineers follow does too.

Professional engineering requires in-depth knowledge of both theory and practice. As Figure 18-2 illustrates, a professional engineer first obtains a Bachelor of Science degree from an accredited engineering school. An engineer then takes a Fundamentals of Engineering (FE) exam, which is sometimes called an Engineer in Training (EIT) exam. After passing the exam, the engineer works for several years under the guidance of a professional engineer. At the end of that period, the engineer takes a professional

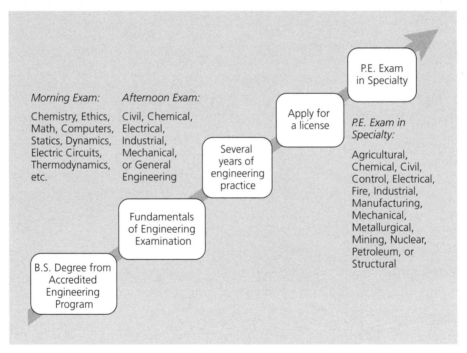

FIGURE 18-2

The occupational development path that professional engineers follow includes education, training, and experience. This provides a good model for professional development in software engineering.

Source: Adapted from Dennis Frailey[5]

engineering exam in his or her specialty area—such as civil, electrical, or chemical engineering. After passing that exam, the engineer's state, province, or territory issues a professional engineer license, and a new Professional Engineer is created.

Striking the right balance between theory and practice in software engineering education depends on making a distinction between education and training. Education seeks to instill qualities in students that will enable them to respond effectively to diverse intellectual challenges. It focuses on general knowledge and includes development of critical thinking skills. Training provides specific skills and knowledge that can be applied immediately and repetitively. Education is strategic; training is tactical.

The most common kind of occupational development for software developers today is training. It tends to be reactive and provided just in time in the specific technologies that a developer needs to know to work on a specific project. Education in longer-lasting software engineering principles is largely absent from the picture. Some people claim that software development has become too specialized and fragmented to be amenable to standardized education. It is too fragmented for standardized training, but not for standardized education.

First Steps

Graduate-level programs in software engineering have existed for about 20 years, but undergraduate programs are still in their infancy, especially in North America. Seattle University awarded the world's first software engineering master's degree in 1982. The Department of Computer Science at the University of Sheffield in the United Kingdom introduced an undergraduate degree program in software engineering in 1988. Rochester Institute of Technology (R.I.T.) initiated the first undergraduate software engineering program in the United States, admitting freshmen in 1996 and graduating its first class in 2001.

At present, about 25 software engineering master's programs are offered in the United States. A handful are offered in Canada, the United Kingdom, Australia, and other countries.[6] As of summer 2003, about two dozen universities offer undergraduate software engineering degrees in the United States and Canada. At least 13 universities offer undergraduate programs in the United Kingdom and at least 6 more offer them in Australia.

R.I.T. and other universities have been working with the IEEE Computer Society, the ACM, and ABET/EAC (Engineering Accreditation Commission) to develop programs that can be accredited as engineering programs in the United States. Figure 18-3 shows an example of the courses required in R.I.T.'s program.

R.I.T.'s Software Engineering Curriculum

First Year
Freshman Seminar (1)*
Computer Science I, II, III (12)
   (fundamentals in computing)
Calculus I, II, III (12)
College Chemistry I (4)
University Physics I, II & Lab (10)
Liberal Arts (12)

Second Year
Engineering of Software Subsystems (4)
Computer Science IV (4) (data structures)
Professional Communications (4)
Introduction to Software Engineering (4)
Assembly Language Programming (4)
Introduction to Digital Systems (4)
Differential Equations (4)
Discrete Mathematics I, II (8)
University Physics III & Lab (5)
Liberal Arts (8)

Third, Fourth, Fifth Years
Principles of Software Architecture (4)
Formal Methods of Specification & Design (4)
Software Requirements & Specification (4)
Software Engineering Project I, II (8)
Scientific Applications Programming (4)
Programming Language Concepts (4)
Computer Organization (4)
Human Factors (4)
Probability & Statistics (4)
Application Domain Electives** (12)
Free Elective (4)
Liberal Arts (18)
Software Design Electives (8)
Software Process Electives (8)
Software Engineering Elective (4)
Cooperative Education (4 quarters required)

*Quarter hours are shown in parentheses.

**Each student must complete a three-course sequence in an application domain related to software engineering. Current domains include Electrical Engineering, Industrial Engineering, Mechanical Engineering, Communications and Networks, Embedded Systems, and Commercial Applications.

FIGURE 18-3

R.I.T.'s undergraduate software engineering program requires courses in computer science, communications, liberal arts, and software engineering.

R.I.T.'s program contains some courses from the computer science department (for example Computer Science I, I, III, and IV). It also contains several courses that you wouldn't normally find in a computer science program, including Engineering of Software Subsystems, Software Requirements & Specification, Software Engineering Project I and II, and Human Factors. It also requires four quarters of cooperative education and significant experience working in teams—in other words, a student must obtain significant experience with industrial practice before earning a degree. This sort of experience requirement is a hallmark of an engineering program. Computer science programs can require industry experience, but only at the expense of diluting their emphasis on pure science.

One interesting aspect of R.I.T.'s program is its length—five years. During the mid-1900s, engineering undergraduate degrees were usually five-year programs.[7] Later, various pressures led universities to shorten their programs to four years. Teaching software engineering as an undergraduate degree in four years may be impractical, especially using the R.I.T. model in which students spend a year gaining experience in industry. Five-year programs may become the norm for undergraduate software engineering.

Accreditation

Accreditation of university programs is required to maintain high standards of software engineering education. Accreditation guarantees that students who graduate from an accredited program will have acquired the basic knowledge of the field. It also ensures that they share a common working vocabulary and common assumptions about good ways to do their work. In the United States, engineering programs are accredited by ABET/EAC, which won't certify a program until it has graduated its first class. Once the first program receives accreditation, many additional universities will likely begin offering software engineering undergraduate programs almost immediately.

One difference between computer science and engineering is the accreditation requirement placed upon faculty who teach those subjects.

The criteria for accrediting computer science programs in the United States require faculty to make "scholarly contributions" to computer science, but they don't require industry experience.[8] In contrast, the ABET/EAC criteria for accrediting engineering programs in the United States state that "non-academic engineering experience" and registration as professional engineers should be considered in faculty evaluations.[9] The CEAB (Canadian Engineering Accreditation Board) uses similar criteria. In professional education, it is important that many of the teachers be qualified and working in the profession—doctors teach doctors; lawyers teach lawyers, and so on.

These differences between engineering and computer science accreditation criteria do not imply that one approach is right and the other is wrong. Their objectives are simply different. Science programs prepare students to conduct research; engineering programs prepare students to participate in industry. Software has a pervasive need for people who have been well prepared to work in industry. Undergraduate degree programs in software engineering are proving to be popular both with students and with the companies that hire them.

Software *Engineering* or *Software* Engineering?

One issue still to be resolved is whether software engineering programs will place a greater emphasis on engineering or on software.

One school of thought, exemplified by the bachelor's program at R.I.T., is that a software engineer should be taught to develop software using a mindset and approaches that have traditionally been associated with engineering, but a software engineer does not necessarily need to be familiar with traditional engineering subjects. This kind of software engineer will take university courses in mathematics, computer science, management, and software-specific topics, but will not take the full set of courses traditionally associated with engineering.

A second school of thought is that a software engineer should be a traditional engineer who has received special training in software development. David Parnas of McMaster University in Ontario, Canada contends that, to achieve full professional credentials and respect from other engineers, professional software engineers need to have the same educational foundation that other engineers have. Software engineers often work in nuclear power plants, avionics software, manufacturing control, and other engineering areas in which knowledge of engineering fundamentals is beneficial or necessary. Students learning this kind of software engineering will take university courses in general chemistry, engineering mathematics, engineering materials, thermodynamics and heat transfer, and other courses that are part of an engineer's traditional core education. They will also take courses that are part of a traditional computer science degree program.

Table 18-1 summarizes the programs of study at McMaster University and R.I.T.[10]

The differences between R.I.T.'s and McMaster's programs point to an important difference in philosophy about software engineering. The McMaster program sees software engineers as engineers who develop software. The R.I.T. program sees software engineers as programmers who create software using an engineering approach.

Programs like the one at McMaster University will produce software engineers who can pass the Fundamentals of Engineering exams that all professional engineers in the United States and Canada must pass and eventually attain a P.E. (professional engineer) license in the United States or a P.Eng. in Canada. Programs like the R.I.T. program won't provide software engineers with the engineering background needed to pass current Fundamentals of Engineering exams.

Both kinds of programs are valuable. The more common need in the software industry is for *software* engineering that produces economical business systems, but the criticality of some systems (including software in nuclear power plants and airplanes) calls equally strongly for software *engineering*. Some people have argued that there is only one true kind of software engineering, but I believe it is appropriate to refer to both kinds of programs as "software engineering" and to the graduates of both kinds of programs as "software engineers."

These different approaches do imply different relations to existing engineering disciplines and different relations to licensing and certification programs. We'll return to these topics in Chapter 19.

TABLE 18-1

Course requirements for two kinds of software engineering

	R.I.T.	MCMASTER U.
Math and Science Chemistry, calculus, matrices, complex numbers differential equations, discrete mathematics, probability and statistics	✓	✓
Introductory Engineering Structure and properties of engineering materials; dynamics and control of physical systems; thermodynamics and heat transfer; waves, electricity and magnetic fields	—	✓
Computer Science Introductory programming; digital system principles; computer architecture; logic design; data structures and algorithms; machine-level programming; programming language concepts; optimization methods, graph models, search and pruning techniques	✓	✓
Software Development Software architecture and design; requirements specification; professional communication skills; designing concurrent and real-time software; designing parallel and distributed systems; computation methods for science and engineering; user interface design	✓	✓
Managing Software Development Software process and product metrics	✓	—
Management Information Systems (MIS) Principles of information systems design	✓	—

Polishing the Badge

After a professional has obtained initial education, gained some experience, and, possibly, received a license, most professions impose a continuing education requirement. The specific requirements for each profession vary from state to state. In Washington State, certified public accountants are required to earn 80 continuing professional education (CPE) credits during the two years preceding renewal of their certificates.[11] Attorneys must obtain 15 continuing legal education (CLE) credits each year. Physicians in New Mexico must obtain 150 hours of continuing education every three years. Engineers in Washington State do not have any continuing education requirements; engineers in some other states do.[12]

Continuing education helps to ensure that professionals stay current in their fields, which is especially important in fields with rapidly changing knowledge such as medicine and software engineering. If professionals stop learning after completing their initial education, time will render their education less and less meaningful.

Continuing-education requirements can be focused so that professionals are required to learn about important developments in their fields. If software engineering ever does discover a new silver bullet, continuing-education requirements can ensure that all licensed or certified software engineers learn about it.

Some Perspective

The field of software engineering is only about 50 years old. In that time, software has managed to revolutionize modern living to such an extent that we have a hard time imagining life without software. As has been the case in other engineering disciplines, software practice has led software theory much of the time, and universities have not always kept up. On the other hand, practice has also had trouble keeping up with some of the theory because the general level of education in software engineering techniques has been so lacking. Without the university infrastructure in place, it's difficult to transfer proven theories into practice.

Educational programs for software engineering that are modeled on traditional engineering programs are just right. They will produce graduates more useful to industry than computer science programs do. They will allow computer science programs to heal their currently split personalities and focus more on science. And a software engineering education will be less painful for all involved than equivalent education from the school of hard knocks.

Notes

1. Jones, Capers, "Gaps in Programming Education," *IEEE Computer,* April 1995, pp. 70–71.

2. Ford, Gary, and Norman E. Gibbs, "A Mature Profession of Software Engineering," SEI, CMU, CMU/SEI-96-TR-004, January 1996.

3. *USA Today,* February 16, 1998, pp. 1B–2B. "Software Jobs Go Begging," *The New York Times,* January 13, 1998, p. A1.

4. The data used to create this graph is from "Table 255.—Bachelor's degrees conferred by degree-granting institutions, by discipline division: 1970–71 to 1999–2000," National Center for Education Statistics, *2001 Digest of Educational Statistics,* Document Number NCES 2002130, April 2002.

5. Dennis Frailey, private communication.

6. For current information, see my company's Web site at www.construx.com/profession.

7. Ford, Gary, and Norman E. Gibbs, "A Mature Profession of Software Engineering," SEI, CMU, CMU/SEI-96-TR-004, January 1996.

8. Criteria for Accrediting Computing Programs: Effective for Evaluations During the 2003–2004 Accreditation Cycle," Computing Accreditation Commission (CAC) of the Accreditation Board for Engineering and Technology, Inc. (ABET), Baltimore, MD, November 2, 2002.

9. "Criteria for Accrediting Engineering Programs," Accreditation Board for Engineering and Technology, Inc., November 1, 1998.

10. The McMaster curriculum can be accessed at www.cas.mcmaster.ca/cas/undergraduate. The R.I.T. program can be accessed at www.se.rit.edu.

11. "Washington Society of Certified Public Accountants Online," www.wscpa.org.

12. "Continuing Education Workshop," *The Washington Board Journal,* Board, Winter/Spring 1999, p. 10.

CHAPTER NINETEEN

Stinking Badges

Badges? We ain't got no badges. We don't need no badges.
I don't have to show you any stinking badges.

GOLD HAT BANDITO,
THE TREASURE OF THE SIERRA MADRE

Few issues are as controversial to software developers as the issues of licensing and certification. Most of the discussion about these issues creates far more heat than light. Misunderstandings of the distinction between licensing and certification are rampant. Will you have to be certified? Will you have to be licensed? How will these issues affect you? This chapter addresses these questions.

Certification

Certification is a *voluntary* process administered by a professional society. The intent of certification is to give the public a way of knowing who is qualified to perform specific kinds of work. Certification requirements usually include both education and experience. In most cases, a written examination is used to determine the competency of the individual seeking certification. Certification usually extends beyond a limited geographic area to national or international regions. The best-known example of professional certification in the United States is Certified Public Accountants.

Some organizations have offered certification for software workers for many years. The Institute for Certification of Computing Professionals offers

Associate Computing Professional and Certified Computing Professional designations. The American Society for Quality Control offers a Software Quality Engineer designation (although their usage of the term "engineer" may expose them to legal problems because that term is regulated by most states[1] and throughout Canada).

Many companies offer certification programs related to specific technologies. Microsoft offers a "Microsoft Certified Professional" designation. Novell offers a "Certified Network Engineer," Oracle offers an "Oracle Certified Professional," and Apple Computer offers an "Apple Certified Server Engineer" designation. The focus of these certifications is limited to a single company's products, which makes them software technologist certifications rather than software engineering certifications.

Certification offers employers and customers a way to recognize software personnel who have achieved at least some minimum level of qualifications. The market is already supporting this claim. At the time I write this, Amazon.com lists 25 *categories* of books on various kinds of software-related and computer-related certification exams. Nearly all of these exams are related to specific technologies.

In 2002, the IEEE Computer Society launched a software engineering fundamentals-based certification called the Certified Software Development Professional.[2] This is the first general software engineering certification sponsored by a major professional organization and is a significant step toward industry-recognized credentialing of software development professionals.

Licensing

Licensing is a *mandatory,* legal process that is intended to protect the public, and is typically administered by jurisdictions (states, provinces, and territories). For many professions, national organizations advise the jurisdictions on appropriate licensing requirements and exam contents.

Most professions are licensed, including doctors, architects, lawyers, and engineers. No occupation that affects the public as much as software

TABLE 19-1
Sample of occupations requiring licenses in California[3]

• Acupuncturist	• Hearing aid dispenser
• Alarm company operator	• Jockey
• Amateur boxer	• Locksmith
• Architect	• Manicurist
• Attorney	• Mule jockey
• Barber	• Nurse
• Certified public accountant	• Pest control operator
• Contractor	• Physician
• Cosmetologist	• Physician's assistant
• Custom upholsterer	• Private investigator
• Dentist	• Professional engineer
• Embalmer	• Real estate appraiser
• Family counselor	• Repossessor
• Funeral director	• Retail furniture dealer
• Geologist	• Veterinarian
• Guide dog instructor	

does remains unlicensed. Table 19-1 lists examples of occupations that require licenses in the state of California.

In engineering in the United States, the majority of engineers are not required to obtain licenses. Engineering companies are required to employ some licensed engineers, but not all of their engineers have to be licensed. About half of civil engineers are licensed, but only eight percent of chemical engineers are licensed. The difference lies in how replicable the engineered artifact is and how much impact the item has on public safety. Artifacts that are replicated in large numbers can be tested before they are manufactured and sold to the public; this generally minimizes the risk to the public and reduces the number of licensed engineers needed for that kind of work. Electrical engineers design artifacts that are reproduced in large quantities—toasters, televisions, telephones, and so on. Thus, only a small percentage of electrical engineers are licensed, as shown in Table 19-2.

TABLE 19-2

Percentage of licensed engineering graduates in the United States as of 1996[4]

DISCIPLINE	LICENSED
Civil	44%
Mechanical	23%
Electrical	9%
Chemical	8%
All Engineers	18%

Civil engineers design many one-of-a-kind artifacts that are also safety-critical—highways, bridges, baseball stadiums, airport runways, and so on. So, as Table 19-2 shows, many more civil engineers than electrical engineers are licensed.

Where would software fit into this table? Software developers produce many one-of-a-kind artifacts, but we also produce operating systems, tax preparation software, word processors, and other programs that are replicated by the millions. We produce some safety-critical systems, but many more business systems with less significant impacts on the public safety.

When a builder remodels a house, the builder can make many design decisions on his own. Occasionally a decision will affect the structural integrity of the house, and the builder will need to have an engineer review those plans. In software, even on applications that require some engineering, much of the work can be done by builders—non-licensed software engineers and software technologists. Thus most software applications do not require any engineering at all, and the applications that do require some engineering will require only a small percentage of the software staff to be licensed software engineers.

When all the dust settles, my best estimate is that fewer than five percent of people currently practicing as computer programmers will eventually need to get their professional engineer licenses in software—and the ratio could easily be closer to one percent.[5]

Can Software Engineers Be Licensed?

Some experts in computer science have argued that licensing would not work or would even be counterproductive.[6] These arguments are repeated often enough to bear examination.

Some arguments focus on the claim that software engineering licensing is impossible or impractical, and some focus on the claim that licensing is simply a bad idea.

Here is a summary of the arguments that licensing is impossible or impractical:

- There is no generally agreed upon body of knowledge for software engineering.[7]
- Knowledge in software engineering changes so quickly that exams will be out of date by the time they're offered.[8]
- No reasonable test for software engineering skill could be put into a multiple-choice format. Indeed, no exam-based practices could adequately ensure competency of software engineers.[9]
- The breadth of subdisciplines involved in developing software would make licensing all of the subdisciplines impractical.[10]
- The Fundamentals of Engineering Exam required for licensing existing professional engineers is inappropriate for those receiving a computer science degree.[11]

Let's take a look at each of these issues in turn.

There is no generally agreed upon body of knowledge for software engineering.

While this claim might have been true 30 years ago, this claim is not true today. As I discussed in Chapter 5, the body of knowledge for software engineering is well defined and fairly stable.

Knowledge in software engineering changes so quickly that exams will be out of date by the time they're offered.

This claim is based on an outdated understanding of what constitutes software engineering's body of knowledge, as discussed in Chapter 5.

Knowledge in some other fields—notably medicine—changes at least as fast as it does in software. If it's possible to license physicians, it's possible to license software engineers.

No reasonable test for software engineering skill could be put into a multiple-choice format. Indeed, no exam-based practices could adequately ensure competency of software engineers.

Creating a meaningful professional-level exam is indeed a challenge. However, the science and statistics of exam creation in support of professional competency recognition is a mature field. Professions ranging from medicine and law to actuarial science and other engineering disciplines all depend on examinations. Exam creation is time consuming, it is labor intensive, and it requires exam creators who are experts. Software engineering exam creation is challenging—as I discovered personally when I helped create the Certified Software Development Professional exam[12]— but it is not any more challenging than it has been for any other profession.

The breadth of subdisciplines involved in developing software would make licensing all of the subdisciplines impractical.

The diversity of software development styles does present a challenge to licensing software engineers. Fortunately, the challenge is simplified because most engineers in software, like most engineers in other disciplines, will not need to be licensed. Only those engineers working on software that poses potential risks to the public's health or welfare would need to be licensed.

The issue of "breadth of subdisciplines" is not unique to software. Physicians take board exams in the areas of cardiology, radiology, oncology, and other specialties. Engineers take specialty exams in civil engineering, electrical engineering, chemical engineering, and so on. If other fields can overcome this obstacle, then eventually so can software.

All things considered, I think this argument is less against licensing and more for setting realistic expectations about what licensing can accomplish in isolation. In other engineering disciplines, engineers are bound by a code of conduct not to practice outside their areas of expertise. Software engineering will need a similar standard of practice.

The Fundamentals of Engineering Exam required for licensing existing professional engineers is inappropriate for those receiving a computer science degree.

The Fundamentals of Engineering exam is currently focused on engineering fundamentals including structure and properties of engineering materials, dynamics and control of physical systems, thermodynamics and heat transfer, magnetic fields, and so on. As I discussed in Chapter 17, some emerging software engineering programs do in fact require students to study these traditional engineering subjects. Other programs focus more on software and less on traditional engineering subjects, and students who graduate from those programs will not be prepared for the FE exam.

There is no doubt that significant work must be done before software engineering licensing can become a reality. But much of that work has been completed at this point, or has been underway for years. In my view, the arguments about licensing's practicality are a sideshow; the real arguments have to with whether licensing is a good idea.

Is Licensing a Bad Idea?

Here is a summary of the arguments that licensing is a bad idea:

- Licenses would unduly restrict the number of people who could practice software engineering at a time when demand for software engineers is increasing.[13]
- When an engineer receives a license, it will be good for life, which is inappropriate considering that software engineering's body of knowledge is changing so rapidly.[14]
- Licensing can't guarantee that every individual who's licensed will actually be competent. Licensing will give the public a false sense of security.[15]

Let's take a closer look at these arguments.

Licenses would unduly restrict the number of people who could practice software engineering at a time when demand for software engineers is increasing.

This argument is based upon the assumption that after licensing is in place only licensed software engineers will be allowed to produce software. As I mentioned earlier in this chapter, that is not how licensing works in other engineering disciplines, and it is not how it would work in software. Most people writing software will be classified as software technologists or unlicensed software engineers, not as professional software engineers. Most kinds of software are not safety critical and can be written by someone other than a professional software engineer.

Only a small number of software engineers who work on specific kinds of safety-critical software systems would ever be required to have licenses.

When an engineer receives a license, it will be good for life, which is inappropriate considering that software engineering's body of knowledge is changing so rapidly.

This argument is based on two misunderstandings of software engineering licensing. The first misunderstanding has to do with how rapidly the body of knowledge is changing, as discussed in Chapter 5. The second misunderstanding is the idea that "licensing" is "licensing for life." Licensees in other fields are required to stay current by obtaining continuing professional education to maintain their licenses. Licensing *supports* keeping professionals up to date.

Licensing can't guarantee that every individual who's licensed will actually be competent. Licensing will give the public a false sense of security.

The argument that some less-qualified people might obtain licenses and some more-qualified people might be denied licenses contains a grain of truth. Licensing acts as a filter that improves the quality of the labor pool, but it is not perfect. Figure 19-1 shows what the labor pool without professional licensing looks like.

Without professional licensing, the public is exposed to both good and bad software development practices and is unprotected against potentially dangerous software. To protect the public interest, we would like the licens-

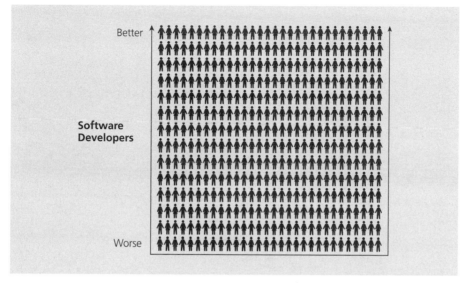

FIGURE 19-1
Pool of all software developers before the filter of professional licensing is applied.

ing procedure to act as a filter that denies licenses to the worst software developers and grants licenses only to the best, as shown in Figure 19-2.

Realistically, licensing will not be an ideal filter. We've all heard of good and bad attorneys, good and bad doctors, and good and bad practitioners from other licensed professions. Even with the combination of university education, exams, and experience, the software-licensing filter won't be any better than filters for existing professions. Initially, it is likely to be worse because other professions have had more time to fine-tune their licensing exams and other requirements. As Figure 19-3 illustrates, even with the best current approaches, software licensing will allow a few unqualified people into the field and will exclude a few who should have been licensed.

Ideal licensing might not be attainable, but realistic licensing can still be valuable. Most software employers would rather choose their software developers from the pool in Figure 19-3 than from the pool in Figure 19-1. Most members of the general public would rather have their safety-critical software designed and checked by developers from the pool in Figure 19-3

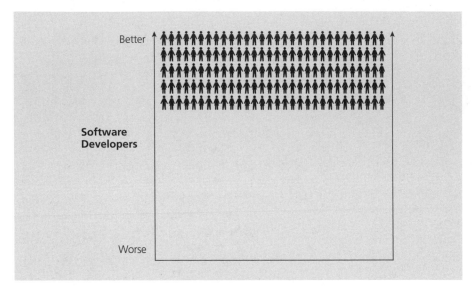

FIGURE 19-2

Pool of software developers after professional licensing has been applied—assuming ideal licensing.

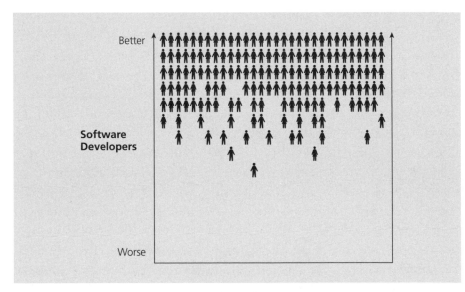

FIGURE 19-3

Pool of software developers after professional licensing has been applied—assuming realistic licensing.

than from the pool in Figure 19-1. Guarantees are nice when you can get them. When guarantees are not possible, more assurance is still better than less.

Bootstrap Licensing

The movement to license software developers began in earnest in 1998, when the Texas Board of Professional Engineers adopted software engineering as a distinct licensable engineering discipline, resulting in a professional engineer or "P.E." designation for professional engineers specializing in software.[16]

In lieu of a recognized exam, Texas began licensing professional software engineers under a restrictive exam-waiver clause. To obtain a P.E. license before the exam becomes available, an applicant must have

- 16 years of engineering experience, or
- 12 years of engineering experience and a bachelor's degree from an accredited university program.
- In addition, each applicant must provide at least nine references, at least five of which must be from licensed professional engineers (not necessarily software engineers).

The same criteria for waiving the professional engineering exam apply to other engineering disciplines in Texas.

How many practicing software developers could qualify as professional software engineers under Texas's current licensing procedure? About 50 have been licensed as of mid-2003, which is not very many, and that's one of the smartest things the state of Texas has done. The natural tendency would be to make the exam-waiver clause so loose during the bootstrapping phase that most current practitioners would automatically qualify. The net effect of that would be to degrade the term "professional software engineer" to mean the same as "run of the mill programmer." By making its exam-waiver clause restrictive, Texas has maximized the likelihood that professional software engineers will represent some of the best software developers in Texas, and it has safeguarded the reputation of the "professional software engineer" title.

Similar developments have been occurring in Canada. The provinces of British Columbia and Ontario began granting professional engineering licenses in software in 1999, and Ontario has licensed about 300 professional software engineers.[17] Like Texas's program, the license programs in both provinces contain bootstrapping provisions to allow software developers with appropriate educations and experiences to obtain professional engineering licenses while examinations are being developed.

Your Stake

One of the consequences of being a professional engineer is that you can be held personally liable for the work your company performs under your signature. Courts in the United States have held that only members of a profession can be found guilty of malpractice.[18] Doctors, lawyers, and architects can be guilty of malpractice. Garbage truck drivers, short order cooks, and computer programmers cannot be guilty of malpractice because, legally, they aren't considered to be professionals. By establishing software engineering as a profession, we are paving the way for the courts to find that software engineers can be held liable for malpractice just like other professionals. On the other hand, following commonly accepted engineering practices could be a defense in some cases.

No individual engineer will be required to be licensed, but some companies eventually will be required to employ licensed engineers. The companies most likely to be required to employ professional engineers include companies that:

- Sell software engineering services to the public
- Perform software work for public agencies
- Produce safety-critical software

Other companies may voluntarily employ professional engineers to take advantage of the marketing cachet of hiring workers with the best available credentials or because they see hiring professional engineers as a way to strengthen their technical talent pool. Hiring software engineers who have obtained certification but not professional engineering status might serve these companies' interests about as well.

Professional engineers in these companies will review software engineering work and sign off on the software their companies deliver. To those companies, employing professional engineers will be a legal necessity. If software companies follow other engineering disciplines, the company that hires a professional engineer will pay for liability insurance as part of the professional engineer's employment package, which will minimize that disadvantage of getting your professional engineering license.

Professional engineers will gain other benefits. The professional engineers who put their signature and reputation on the line for their companies will have final say over methodology choices, design approaches, and other decisions that affect the quality of the software for which they might be held liable. Without professional standing, your boss can come to you and demand that you commit to an unrealistic schedule, make shortsighted design compromises, or sacrifice quality in order to get the software out the door. With a well-defined profession—consisting of education, a code of ethics, and licensing—you will be able to say, "The standards of my profession don't allow me to shortchange quality in this situation. I could lose my license or get sued." You will have a professional and legal basis for standing up to unenlightened managers, marketers, and customers—a basis that is sorely lacking today.

At the organizational level, we may see an interplay between an organization's SW-CMM rating (discussed in Chapter 14) and the professional engineering license. Professional engineers will potentially be liable for the software written under their supervision. Professional engineers won't be able to personally review every line of code on large projects. Even if the organization pays for professional engineers' liability policy, I think that professional engineers will generally want to work for organizations in which they receive the best technical and process support, in other words, which have the most sophisticated software organizational infrastructure. I predict that we'll see a concentration of professional engineers in organizations that have achieved higher SW-CMM levels. This will reinforce the phenomenon that Harlan Mills observed 20 years ago: above-average developers tend to cluster in effective organizations and below-average developers in ineffective organizations.[19]

Earning the Badge

A key step in any mature licensing plan is a competency exam administered by each jurisdiction, and the form of software's professional engineer exam has not yet been determined. In other branches of engineering, professional engineers generally take an eight-hour exam that includes solving eight problems—four are answered in essay format and four require about ten multiple-choice answers each. The specifics vary from jurisdiction to jurisdiction.

Exams by themselves aren't foolproof, and passing the software professional engineer exam by itself will not be sufficient to obtain a license. A professional engineering license traditionally requires both work experience and a degree from an accredited engineering school. In software engineering, the degree is problematic because, although about a dozen universities now offer undergraduate programs in software engineering, none have yet been accredited in the United States, though three programs have been accredited in Canada.[20] Accreditation of the first program in the United States is expected in 2003 shortly after publication of this book. We can expect a non-degree bootstrap-licensing phase to last 10 to 15 years until the university infrastructure is in place to graduate sufficient numbers of software engineers.

Three Paths

As I discussed in Chapter 18, the software community has not yet resolved whether a software engineer is an engineer who develops software or a programmer who creates software by using an engineering approach. The differences between these two schools of thought about software engineering suggest that licensing will eventually progress along one of three paths.

The first path involves creating a specialty exam in software within the framework of traditional engineering licensing. Engineers who have passed the Fundamentals of Engineering exam and obtained the required work experience could obtain their P.E./P.Eng. in software by passing the software engineering specialty exam. This path would require software engineers to be educated in programs like the one at McMaster University, described in Chapter 18.

The second path again involves creating a software engineering specialty exam, but it also entails modifying the Fundamentals of Engineering exams taken by all engineers (the specific exams vary by jurisdiction). Most engineers today use computers extensively, and many create computer programs for their own use or for use by their colleagues. These programs are used to provide data used in the design of bridges, skyscrapers, oil refineries, and many other structures that potentially impact the public welfare. The engineers writing these programs should have knowledge of effective software engineering practices. The Fundamentals of Engineering exams might simply need to be revised to contain a higher percentage of questions about software engineering. The exams are designed to be broad, and the score required to pass is fairly low—usually around 70 percent, although it varies by jurisdiction. Engineers trained in other disciplines will get more software answers wrong and traditional engineering answers right; software engineers will get more software answers right and traditional engineering answers wrong. This path could be taken by engineers who have been educated in programs like the one at R.I.T., described in Chapter 18.

The third path would involve creating a professional credential that is more software specific than a traditional P.E./P.Eng.: "Professional Software Engineer (P.S.E.)" or some such label. Obtaining this credential would focus solely on software and would not require education in thermodynamics and heat transfer, properties of engineering materials, or other traditional engineering topics. An argument in favor of this approach is that people designing business systems, financial applications, educational programs, and other software that isn't used for engineering purposes really don't need knowledge of traditional engineering topics, but would still benefit from learning an engineering approach to building software.

Of these three options, I think the second path is the best approach. Software engineers should take enough traditional engineering courses to understand how engineers in various disciplines think about design and problem solving, and the third path doesn't require that. But engineers don't need to take every traditional engineering course to learn the engineering mindset, and the first path requires too much of that. Moreover, only a minority of software engineers will ever be licensed, and software engineering curriculum should be based on the reality that most graduates will not need to be prepared for the Fundamentals of Engineering exam. For those software engineers who do decide to become licensed, the second path will prepare them to pass a revised Fundamentals of Engineering exam without excessively diluting coursework specific to software engineering.

Would changing the Fundamentals of Engineering exam be good for other engineering disciplines? I think so. Changing the Fundamentals of Engineering exams wouldn't reduce the caliber of engineers who are eventually granted licenses. Those engineers will still need to pass their engineering specialty exams at the end of their Engineer in Training period—whether in civil engineering, chemical engineering, aeronautical engineering, or another specialty. Engineers' ethics codes prohibit them from practicing in fields outside their areas of expertise. In addition, software is so pervasive in modern engineering that introducing *all* engineers to software engineering might provide a significant benefit: it could cause them to understand the challenges associated with creating complex software systems and to recognize when they need to bring in expert help for projects that are beyond the scope of their education and training.

Stinking Badges or an Iron Ring?

In Canada, engineers who graduate from an accredited engineering program receive an iron ring at graduation time. Since 1923, the ring has been awarded in a secret ceremony that was developed by Rudyard Kipling.

Tradition holds that these rings are made from the iron of a bridge that collapsed, and engineers wear the ring on their working hand as a reminder of their responsibility to society. Attempts have been made to bring the tradition of the iron ring to engineers in the United States, but so far the practice is not widespread.

The iron ring is significant because, even though it doesn't designate full professional status, it does symbolize a commitment to engineering as a career. Certification may play a similar role in software—symbolizing a commitment to high standards of software engineering.

If you think, "We don't need no stinking badges or iron ring," you're right. The majority of software developers will choose not to attain their professional engineering licenses—their badges—even after licensing becomes widespread. The majority probably won't attain certification either. But as the software engineering field matures, both licensing and certification will become more prominent. A software engineer who wants to demonstrate a commitment to the software profession will have the option to get a license, a certification, or both.

Notes

1. Kaner, Cem, "Computer Malpractice," *Software QA,* vol. 3, no. 4, 1997, p. 23.

2. See www.computer.org/certification for details.

3. Ford, Gary, and Norman E. Gibbs, "A Mature Profession of Software Engineering," SEI, CMU, CMU/SEI-96-TR-004, January 1996.

4. Ford, Gary, and Norman E. Gibbs, "A Mature Profession of Software Engineering," SEI, CMU, CMU/SEI-96-TR-004, January 1996.

5. Ford and Gibbs make a similar point—they estimate that fewer than 10 percent of software workers will receive licenses. Ford, Gary, and Norman E. Gibbs, "A Mature Profession of Software Engineering," SEI, CMU, CMU/SEI-96-TR-004, January 1996.

6. Knight, John C., and Nancy Leveson, "Should Software Engineers Be Licensed?" *Communications of the ACM,* November 2002, pp. 87–90. White, John, and Barbara Simons, "ACM's Position on Licensing of Software Engineers," *Communications of the ACM,* November 2002, p. 91. Kennedy, Ken, and Moshe Y. Vardi, "A Rice University Perspective on Software Engineering Licensing," *Communications*

of the ACM, November 2002, pp. 94–95. McCalla, Gord, "Software Engineering Requires Individual Professionalism," *Communications of the ACM,* November 2002, pp. 98–101. DeMarco, Tom, "Certification or Decertification," *Communications of the ACM,* July 1999, p. 11.

7. Knight, John C., and Nancy Leveson, "Should Software Engineers Be Licensed?" *Communications of the ACM,* November 2002, pp. 87–90.

8. Knight, John C., and Nancy Leveson, "Should Software Engineers Be Licensed?" *Communications of the ACM,* November 2002, pp. 87–90. McCalla, Gord, "Software Engineering Requires Individual Professionalism," *Communications of the ACM,* November 2002, pp. 98–101.

9. Knight, John C., and Nancy Leveson, "Should Software Engineers Be Licensed?" *Communications of the ACM,* November 2002, pp. 87–90.

10. Knight, John C., and Nancy Leveson, "Should Software Engineers Be Licensed?" *Communications of the ACM,* November 2002, pp. 87–90. McCalla, Gord, "Software Engineering Requires Individual Professionalism," *Communications of the ACM,* November 2002, pp. 98–101.

11. Knight, John C., and Nancy Leveson, "Should Software Engineers Be Licensed?" *Communications of the ACM,* November 2002, pp. 87–90. White, John, and Barbara Simons, "ACM's Position on Licensing of Software Engineers," *Communications of the ACM,* November 2002, p. 91.

12. See www.computer.org/certification.

13. Kennedy, Ken, and Moshe Y. Vardi, "A Rice University Perspective on Software Engineering Licensing," *Communications of the ACM,* November 2002, pp. 94–95.

14. McCalla, Gord, "Software Engineering Requires Individual Professionalism," *Communications of the ACM,* November 2002, pp. 98–101.

15. Knight, John C., and Nancy Leveson, "Should Software Engineers Be Licensed?" *Communications of the ACM,* November 2002, pp. 87–90.

16. www.tbpe.state.tx.us.

17. Parnas, David Lorge, "Licensing Software Engineers in Canada," *Communications of the ACM,* November 2002, pp. 96–98.

18. Kaner, Cem, "Computer Malpractice," *Software QA,* Volume 3, no. 4, 1997, p. 23.

19. Mills, Harlan D., *Software Productivity,* Boston, MA: Little, Brown, 1983, pp. 71–81.

20. Parnas, David Lorge, "Licensing Software Engineers in Canada," *Communications of the ACM,* November 2002, pp. 96–98.

CHAPTER TWENTY

The Professional's Code

*Although there is a little bit of Peter Pan in each of us,
maturity brings with it the desire to contribute to the communal welfare. The fulfillment of this yearning, I repeat,
provides the engineer with his primary existential pleasure.*

SAMUEL C. FLORMAN

One of the signs of a mature profession is the presence of a code of
ethics or standard of professional conduct. Legally, professionals
are held to a higher standard for their work than nonprofessionals performing work in the same field. If your friend the plumber tells you to take
Alka-Seltzer for a stomachache and the problem turns out to be a ruptured
appendix, the plumber hasn't done anything unethical. If your friend were
a doctor and told you the same thing without conducting an adequate
examination, that doctor's advice would be an unethical act.

A code of ethics establishes the standard of conduct for each profession.[1] Certified Public Accountants are required to pass a three-hour exam
covering the accounting code of ethics. Lawyers are required to pass a half-
day ethics exam. In mature professions, workers can be disbarred or lose
their licenses for serious violations of their ethics codes.

A Code for Coders

Software development survived for many years without a widely
accepted code of ethics. In the late 1990s, a joint committee of the ACM

and IEEE Computer Society began developing a code of ethics for software engineering. The Code underwent several drafts and was reviewed by practicing software developers worldwide. In 1998, the Software Engineering Code of Ethics and Professional Practice was adopted by both the ACM and IEEE Computer Society. The Code is reproduced in Figure 20-1. A more detailed version of the Code is also available and is accessible from the IEEE Computer Society Web site at www.computer.org.

The Code is based on two overriding goals stated in the preamble and eight specific principles enumerated in the Code's detailed paragraphs.

The Software Engineering Code of Ethics and Professional Practice

Software engineers shall commit themselves to making the analysis, specification, design, development, testing, and maintenance of software a beneficial and respected profession. In accordance with their commitment to the health, safety and welfare of the public, software engineers shall adhere to the following eight principles:

1. **Public** Software engineers shall act consistently with the public interest.

2. **Client and Employer** Software engineers shall act in a manner that is in the best interests of their client and employer consistent with the public interest.

3. **Product** Software engineers shall ensure that their products and related modifications meet the highest professional standards possible.

4. **Judgment** Software engineers shall maintain integrity and independence in their professional judgment.

5. **Management** Software engineering managers and leaders shall subscribe to and promote an ethical approach to the management of software development and maintenance.

6. **Profession** Software engineers shall advance the integrity and reputation of the profession consistent with the public interest.

7. **Colleagues** Software engineers shall be fair to and supportive of their colleagues.

8. **Self** Software engineers shall participate in lifelong learning regarding the practice of their profession and shall promote an ethical approach to the practice of the profession.

FIGURE 20-1

The Software Engineering Code of Ethics and Professional Practice. This Code has been adopted by both the ACM and IEEE Computer Society and provides ethical and professional guidance for software engineers.

© 1998 SEEPP Executive Committee. Used by permission.

The first overriding goal is that "Software engineers shall commit themselves to making the analysis, specification, design, development, testing, and maintenance of software a beneficial and respected profession." In other words, one function of the Code is to foster the development of the software engineering profession itself. This language implicitly acknowledges that software engineering is not yet a "beneficial and respected profession." Once the profession has become more mature, this language may be revised to say that software engineers will "maintain" or "enhance" the respected profession rather than "make" it.

The second overriding goal is that software engineers have a "commitment to the health, safety and welfare of the public." This is consistent with the idea that engineers more commonly have a duty to society than to specific individuals. Other engineering codes of ethics similarly emphasize the importance of protecting public welfare.[2]

These two goals are primary, and the eight specific principles should be interpreted as supporting these overarching goals. Here are some implications of the Code.

1. Public. Software engineers shall accept full responsibility for their work and approve software only if they have a well-founded belief that it is safe, meets specifications, passes appropriate tests, and is ultimately for the public good. Software engineers shall disclose any actual or potential danger to specific persons, the public, or the environment.

2. Client and Employer. Clients and employers are directly affected by software engineers' work, and so software engineers need to protect their clients' and employers' interests, except when their interests conflict with a greater public interest. Software engineers shall provide services only within their areas of expertise. They shall protect confidential information and not accept outside work or promote interests that are detrimental to their clients or employers. They shall not use software that was obtained illegally or unethically. If they think a project is likely to fail, they shall report the evidence that leads them to believe that to their employer or client.

3. Product. In all their work, software engineers shall strive for high quality, acceptable costs, and reasonable schedules. They shall ensure that tradeoffs among these are clear to their employers and clients. They shall provide assessments of the uncertainties contained in their estimates. Software engineers shall follow relevant professional standards. They shall ensure that software has been adequately reviewed and tested before it is released to the public.

4. Judgment. True professionals have both the right and the duty to exercise their professional judgment independently—to adhere to a high professional standard even when it conflicts with their self-interest or their clients' or employers' interests. Software engineers shall endorse only products that they have adequately reviewed and objectively agree with. They shall not engage in illegal or dishonest activities such as bribery, double billing, or working for two parties that have conflicting interests without fully disclosing the conflict of interest.

5. Management. Software engineering managers shall abide by the same professional standards as other software engineers, including the provisions of the Code of Ethics. Software engineering managers shall treat their employees fairly and honestly. They shall assign work to people qualified to perform the work, tempered with the goal of furthering each employee's education and experience. They shall ensure realistic quantitative estimates of cost, schedule, staffing, quality, and other outcomes of projects they work on.

6. Profession. Software engineers shall help to advance software engineering as a profession. They shall promote public knowledge of software engineering. They shall create a work environment that supports the Code and refuse to work for organizations that are in conflict with the Code. They shall report significant violations of the Code to colleagues, managers, or other appropriate authorities.

7. Colleagues. Software engineers shall help other software engineers follow the Code of Ethics. They shall treat each other fairly, and provide assistance in others' professional development. In situations that require expertise outside their areas of competence, they shall call upon the assistance of other professionals who have appropriate expertise.

8. Self. Software engineers shall make self-education a career-long priority. They shall maintain current knowledge of developments in software requirements, design, construction, maintenance, testing, and management. They shall maintain current knowledge of standards and laws relevant to their work.

Benefits of the Code of Ethics

A recognized Code of Ethics provides broad support for a true profession of software engineering. It establishes minimum performance expectations. It gives employers and clients confidence about the professional standards and character of engineers who adhere to the Code.

The Code provides a way for companies to show their support for professional software engineering. When a company commits to the Code, it commits to providing an environment in which professional software engineers can make ethical conduct a priority without jeopardizing their advancement within that company. This is beneficial both to the company and to the software engineers it employs. The company attracts software engineers with high professional standards, and its engineers find professional fulfillment in an environment that appreciates their high standards.

Some of the strongest benefits of the Code arise from the guidance it provides for software engineers' ethical and professional conduct, guidance that has been sorely lacking. Consider the following cases:

- *Death-march projects.* Without a code of ethics, software engineers who believe a project's schedule is unachievable might debate whether to report that to their client or manager. With the Code, if software engineers think a project is likely to fail, they should collect evidence and document their concerns. The Code says they have a professional duty to report their concerns promptly to their employer or client.

- *Low-ball bidding.* The practice of submitting unrealistically low bids to clients is common in the software industry. Software developers might not like the practice, but many feel uncomfortable defying their bosses by refusing to support a low-ball bid. The Code states that software engineers should ensure that estimates are realistic and should not endorse documents unless they agree with them. It also calls upon software engineers to make software engineering a respected profession, a goal that is undermined by participating in low-ball bidding. The ethical software engineer should refuse to endorse low-ball bids.

- *Code-and-fix development.* Uninformed clients and managers sometimes insist that software developers engage in code-and-fix development. Software developers know that code-and-fix development is ineffective, but, after repeated battles with clients and managers, many finally sigh, "I'll let this company get the results it deserves." Use of code-and-fix development, however, is inconsistent with a software engineer's ethical duty to produce high-quality products for acceptable costs and within reasonable schedules. Continued use of code-and-fix development also undermines the advancement of software engineering as a profession, and ethical software engineers should refuse to use code-and-fix development.

- *Knowledge stagnation.* Keeping up to date in software engineering can be time-consuming, and many software developers don't even try. One publisher reported that the average software developer reads less than one professional book each year and subscribes to no professional magazines.[3] This might not seem like an ethical issue, but it is certainly a *professional practice* issue. A person cannot perform at a professional level without keeping current in the knowledge of the profession. A person who doesn't want to engage in ongoing self-education can continue to perform software work at some level, but according to the Code of Ethics and Professional

Practice, a person cannot be a *professional* software engineer without participating in lifelong learning.

Without a code of ethics, software engineers must rely solely on their individual judgments to resolve ethical dilemmas. Engineers who act consistently with the Code will know that the consensus of engineers is behind them; they don't have to take their ethical stands in isolation.

Some situations will be less clear-cut than the examples listed above. The interests of a client may come into conflict with the public interest. Or the interests of an employer might conflict with the interests of a software engineering colleague. The Code cannot foresee every possible ethical dilemma, and the Code calls for software engineers to use their best ethical judgment to adhere to the spirit of the Code, considering the Code as a whole.

Coming of Age

The Code provides a way of educating the public, including clients and upper management, about what to expect from professional software engineers. Of course, the Code is meaningful only if employers and clients can reasonably expect that software engineering professionals actually follow the Code. Every profession needs a way to discipline workers who fail to live up to the relevant professional standards. Without enforcement, workers who don't live up to the Code can gradually erode the credibility of the profession. At the present time, neither the IEEE Computer Society, the ACM, nor any other organization has any meaningful authority to enforce the Code. Compliance with the Code is voluntary. In the long run, however, software engineering will follow the same path as other professions: full professional standing and adherence to the Code will become a package deal. The Code will be enforced, which will be beneficial to individual software engineers, their employers and clients, and the public.

Samuel Florman said, "maturity brings with it the desire to contribute to the communal welfare." Florman was referring to individuals, but his statement might just as well have referred to the software engineering occupation. The Software Engineering Code of Ethics and Professional Practice, which emphasizes responsibility to the profession and contribution to society as a whole, is one indication that software engineering itself is beginning to grow up.

Notes

1. See, for example, the American Institute of Architects' *Code of Ethics and Professional Conduct* at www.aiaonline.com; the American Institute for Certified Public Accountants' *Code of Professional Conduct* at www.aicpa.org; the National Society of Professional Engineers' *Code of Ethics for Engineers* at www.nspe.org; the American Society of Mechanical Engineers' *Code of Ethics of Engineers* at www.asme.org; and the Institute of Electrical and Electronics Engineers' *Code of Ethics* at www.ieee.org. Current links for each of these ethics codes are available from my company's Web site at www.construx.com/profession.

2. See, for example, the National Society of Professional Engineers' *Code of Ethics for Engineers* at www.nspe.org.

3. Reported in Tom DeMarco and Timothy Lister, *Peopleware: Productive Projects and Teams,* 2d Ed., New York: Dorset House, 1999.

CHAPTER TWENTY-ONE

Alchemy

Q: What are the most exciting/promising software engi-neering ideas or techniques on the horizon?

A: I don't think that the most promising ideas are on the horizon. They are already here and have been here for years but are not being used properly.

DAVID L. PARNAS[1]

How to transmute base metals into gold? That is the perennial question from would-be Midases everywhere. Software engineering is in a unique position to realize the alchemic dream by hastening the adoption of practices that are well understood and that were proved beneficial many years ago, but are still not commonly used. We are in a position to transform the lead of average practice into the gold of best practice.

Why Technology Transfer Is Needed

The software engineering field already has good practices for project planning and management, requirements engineering, design, construction, quality assurance, and process improvement. The problem is that too few practitioners know about the practices, and even fewer people use them. Table 21-1 lists some examples of best practices with which leading software organizations have accumulated a great deal of experience, that are usually successful, and that—as far as I can tell from my consulting experience and various published industry reports—are used by only a slim minority of software organizations.

TABLE 21-1

Software best practices that are rarely used[2]

BEST PRACTICES	YEAR FIRST DESCRIBED IN PRINT OR FIRST COMMERCIALLY AVAILABLE
Project planning and management practices	
• Automated estimation tools	1973[3]
• Evolutionary delivery	1988[4]
• Measurement	1977[5]
• Productivity environments	1984[6]
• Risk management planning	1981[7]
Requirements engineering practices	
• Change board	1978[8]
• Throwaway user interface prototyping	1975[9]
• JAD sessions	1985[10]
Design practices	
• Information hiding	1972[11]
• Design for change	1979[12]
Construction practices	
• Source code control	1980[13]
• Incremental integration	1979[14]
Quality assurance practices	
• Branch-coverage testing	1979[15]
• Inspections	1976[16]
Process improvement	
• Software Engineering Institute's Software Capability Maturity Model	1987[17]
• Software Engineering Process Groups	1989[18]

Researchers have found that it typically takes 10 to 15 years for innovations—new best practices—to flow down the technology-transfer stream into common practice.[19] If that's the case, the software industry's technology transfer cycle is seriously broken. Most of the best practices listed in Table 21-1 have been described in print for 15 years or more. Why aren't they being used?

Diffusion of Innovation

The answer to that question is both easier and harder than you might think. The way in which innovations are diffused into common practice has been studied extensively. The seminal work on technology transfer is Everett M. Rogers's *Diffusion of Innovations,* which was originally published in 1962.[20] In the fourth edition, published in 1995, Rogers comments that more than 3,500 books and articles about diffusion were published between his first edition and his fourth.

Rogers maps out a description of how innovations are adopted based on categorization of the adopters. The adopters include Innovators, Early Adopters, Early Majority, Late Majority, and Laggards. Figure 21-1 shows both the relative sizes of these groups and the sequence in which they adopt innovations.

Innovators are adventurous. They want to try out new technologies, no matter how rash, daring, or risky. They can cope with the high degree of uncertainty brought on by adopting unstable new technologies and practices. Because they court risk, they fail frequently. As a result they may not be respected by people from the other adopter categories.

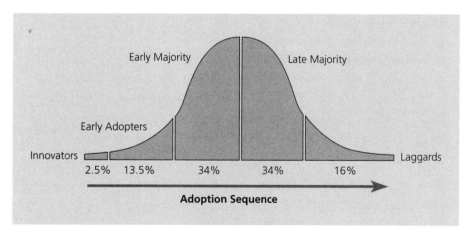

FIGURE 21-1

Innovations are diffused over time. The different groups that adopt an innovation have different needs and use different criteria to evaluate it.

Source: Adapted from *Diffusion of Innovations.*[21]

Early Adopters are the respected opinion leaders in their organizations. They are ahead of the majority in adopting innovations, but just far enough to serve as role models for other adopters.

Adopters in the *Early Majority* are more deliberate about taking up innovations than Early Adopters, and they are one of the two largest groups. Their decision period is longer than the Early Adopters'. They follow the lead the Early Adopters establish.

Adopters in the *Late Majority* are skeptical of innovations. They are cautious and adopt innovations only after many others have already adopted them. They are not convinced that the innovations are better or that they apply to them. Their adoption may depend on being pressured by their peers.

Laggards are the last to adopt innovations and tend to focus more on the past than the future. They are extremely cautious in adopting innovations.

The Chasm

Rogers's work was extended in the mid-1990s by Geoffrey Moore in *Crossing the Chasm.*[22] Moore pointed out that the differences in decision-making styles between the adopter groups create gaps between them. A message that persuades Innovators to adopt something new would not necessarily persuade Early Adopters.

Moore's most significant insight was that not all the gaps are equal. As Figure 21-2 illustrates, Moore believes that the gap between Early Adopters and the Early Majority is much wider than the rest, wide enough that he calls it a chasm.

Some Tough Questions

One reason that new innovations move into practice slowly is that some of them don't work very well in practice! Not all innovations are useful, and the Early Majority, Late Majority, and Laggards have some good reasons for being cautious. When presented with an innovation, they ask tough questions like these:[23]

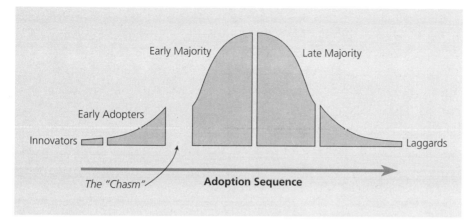

FIGURE 21-2

One difficulty with technology transfer is crossing the chasm that separates the needs of the Early Adopters from the needs of the Early Majority.

Source: Adapted from *Crossing the Chasm.*[24]

- Do experimental results prove conclusively that the innovation will work in practice?
- Are successes a result of the innovation itself, or might they be the result of the people using it?
- Is the innovation complete, or does it need to be adapted or extended before it can be applied?
- Does the innovation have significant overhead (training, documentation) that offsets its value in the long run?
- If the innovation was developed in a research setting, does it apply to real-world problems?
- Does the innovation generally slow down the programmers?
- Can the innovation be misapplied?
- Is information available about the risks involved with using the innovation?
- Does the innovation include information about how to integrate it with existing practices?
- Must the innovation be applied in its entirety to realize significant benefits?

Very few software engineering practices have had data collected and disseminated widely enough to prepare software practitioners to answer questions like these. As a result, the software engineering practices described in Table 21-1 are stuck on the left side of the chasm. Early Adopters have been using many of those techniques for 15 years or more, while the later adopter groups are largely unaware of them. The numbers from Rogers's adopter categories are close to the numbers of projects that use code-and-fix development—about 75 percent of projects are still using code and fix or its close cousins, and a similar percentage of adopters fall onto the right side of the chasm.

Why is this? In Rogers's framework, one reason that innovations are diffused to Innovators and Early Adopters more quickly is that Innovators and Early Adopters tend to have more resources—they are in better positions to afford costly mistakes. Later adopters are more cautious partly because they aren't as resource rich. As I mentioned in Chapter 12, however, the scarce resource in this case isn't money; it's *time*. Lagging-edge practices such as code-and-fix development are associated with significant schedule overruns. The overtime that usually accompanies such overruns doesn't leave time for investigating and adopting more effective innovations.

Where's the Risk?

The conventional wisdom is that if you're a risk taker, you'll be to the left of the chasm. If you're risk averse, you'll be to the right of the chasm. But this conventional wisdom doesn't apply very well to current software engineering.

As Figure 21-3 illustrates, the practices from Table 21-1 are currently being used by Innovators and Early Adopters. The figure also shows a few specific practices to establish some reference points. The SEI's SW-CMM model seems to be crossing the chasm. The well-known waterfall lifecycle model is in Late Majority territory, and code-and-fix development is well into Laggard territory.

The state of the art in software engineering has advanced by leaps and bounds since the 1968 NATO Conference on Software Engineering. But we

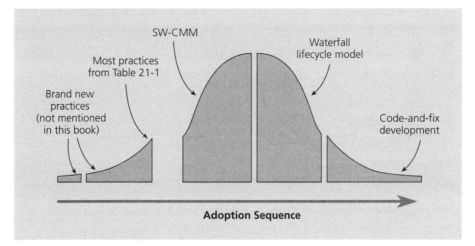

FIGURE 21-3

Different software development practices are at different stages in the innovation adoption sequence. The practices in Table 21-1 are ready to cross the chasm. The SW-CMM is in widespread use in some industries but is virtually unknown in other industries (that is, it has crossed the chasm in some industries but not in others). Older practices such as code-and-fix development are on their way out (or at least they should be).

still find many organizations using practices that are 10 to 20 years out of date—or more—and which could be replaced by better practices. The industry is confronting a problem of slow diffusion. I've mentioned elsewhere that organizations that use these old practices face a high risk of cost overruns, schedule overruns, and project cancellations. I repeat that fact here to emphasize that occupying one of the later adopter roles in the software field *is not currently minimizing risk* for the organizations in those positions. Just as it's possible to spend more on repairs for an old car that keeps breaking down than on payments for a newer one, it's possible to incur more risk by using out-of-date software development practices than by moving to newer, better practices.

Where do you want to be on the technology transfer cycle? As Figure 21-4 illustrates, on the far left, accepting the risk of promising but as-yet-unproved innovations is justified because the innovations might yield high payoffs. On the far right, the risk from using outdated practices is equally high, but there's no potential for high payoffs and the risk isn't justified.

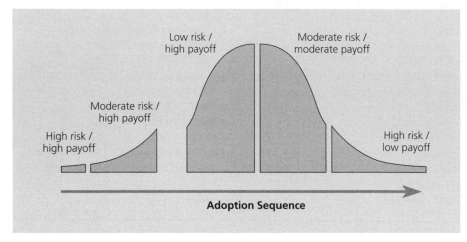

FIGURE 21-4

Considering the rate at which software practices have improved, the traditional innovation risk/reward payoff has gotten out of balance. Both extremes of the innovation adoption curve present high risk.

The software industry is in an unusual technology-transfer situation. Many innovative practices that have proved their value, such as those in Table 21-1, have congregated on the left brink of the chasm. They are ready to cross for organizations that are willing to kick their addiction to code-and-fix development and other kinds of software fool's gold. This situation is unusual because typically the risk of being an Early Adopter would be higher. It's as if leading-edge doctors had tested penicillin, found it to be effective, and integrated it into their practices only to have 75 percent of doctors continue to use leeches and mustard poultices. If you're still using leeches and poultices at the beginning of the 21st century, you're taking on more risk by refusing innovations than by adopting them.

If your organization is currently in the Early Majority, Late Majority, or Laggard categories, you can lower your risk by adopting some of the modern practices listed in Table 21-1. Using code-and-fix development is risky. Using the waterfall model is risky. Adopting the SW-CMM is somewhat risky, but not as risky as these older practices. Industry experience cited throughout this book shows this claim to be true. The difficulty is diffusing the message out into the field.

County Extension Agents

In the area of innovation diffusion, the United States's agricultural extension service is regarded as the most successful program in the world. As one author said, "It is impossible for anyone to speak ten words about diffusion without two of them being 'agricultural extension.'"[25] The service consists of three parts:

- *A Research Subsystem,* consisting of research professors at agricultural experiment stations in each of the 50 states. These professors produce the innovations that are later diffused.
- *State Extension Specialists,* who link the research work to the County Extension Agents.
- *County Extension Agents,* who work with farmers and other people at the local level, helping them to choose innovations appropriate for their needs. They answer practitioners' tough questions such as, "Is the innovation complete, or does it need to be adapted or extended before it can be applied?" and "Are the innovation's successes a result of the innovation itself, or might they be the result of the people using it?"

The agricultural program places a strong emphasis on cooperation among its three parts. Research professors are rewarded for publishing research results in a form directly useful to farmers. State Extension Specialists are evaluated based on how well they relate their technical knowledge to farmers' problems.

The program's annual investment in diffusing agricultural innovation is approximately equal to the annual investment in agricultural research, which makes the program unique. No other Federal program spends more than a few percent of its budget on diffusion, and no other program is as successful at changing common practice.

Experience in the software industry provides some confirmation of the value of emphasizing diffusion. One of the best software organizations, NASA's Software Engineering Laboratory, has found that packaging the results of its measurement and analysis program into guidebooks and training courses is a critical part of its award-winning process-improvement program.[26]

Diffusion of innovation in software is needed, and the software industry does have the beginnings of a diffusion program. The Software Engineering Institute (SEI) was created with Federal funding to "provide leadership in advancing the state of the practice of software engineering to improve the quality of systems that depend on software."[27] The SEI essentially performs the role that the Research Subsystem does in the agricultural diffusion model. At about 300 employees to serve 2.9 million software workers, however, the SEI program is only in the beginning stages compared to the agriculture program, which employs about 17,000 people to serve 3.8 million agricultural workers.[28]

Everett Rogers points out that many government agencies have tried to copy the agricultural extension model but have failed because, among other reasons, they didn't establish local-level change agents analogous to the County Extension Agents. Rogers's analysis goes a long way toward explaining the limited impact that the SEI has had so far on commercial practice. The SEI was created by the United States Department of Defense (DoD), and the documents and materials it has produced have had a strong DoD flavor. Not surprisingly, the industries that benefited earliest from the SEI's technology-transfer role were military contractors and government agencies.[29]

The software industry has many subindustries that have specific needs and specialized vocabularies. These subindustries include business systems, Web development, software products, games, medical devices, systems software, computer manufacturing, embedded systems, aerospace, and many others. Combine the failure to translate software engineering innovations into terms familiar to each specific industry with the common lack of in-depth education in software engineering, and you have a formula for slow progress.

Practitioners won't adopt innovations until they get their tough questions answered in terms they can relate to. For software technology transfer to work effectively, either the government or private industry needs to fund roles similar to the State Extension Specialist and County Extension Agent. Software-project needs don't vary from county to county as farming needs do. But they do vary from subindustry to subindustry, and software engineering might very well benefit from extension specialists who can link general software research to specific subindustries.

Other developments that will help speed technology transfer include the elements of a mature profession I have discussed throughout this book: undergraduate educational programs in software engineering, professional credentialing, requirements for ongoing professional education, organizational certification, and a professional code of conduct.

The Humbling Nature of Progress

A few years ago I traveled to a rural town, not to meet with a County Extension Agent, but to meet with a software engineering colleague I hadn't previously met in person. Immediately after we introduced ourselves, he asked me, "Writing a book the size of *Code Complete* was awfully audacious for someone your age, wouldn't you agree?"

Much as I like being called audacious, I would not agree. My writing of *Code Complete* is representative of the way that knowledge is transferred from generation to generation in scientific and engineering fields, and of the way knowledge ultimately advances. Early pioneers in software engineering such as Victor Basili, Barry Boehm, Larry Constantine, Bill Curtis, Tom DeMarco, Tom Gilb, Capers Jones, Harlan Mills, David Parnas, and others struggle to create leading-edge concepts from ill-defined bits of knowledge. They work against backgrounds of erroneous theories, conflicting data, and sketchy or nonexistent previous work. Later, others have the benefit of reading the early pioneers' work, and they are not exposed to all the false turns and mistaken assumptions. Newcomers who haven't struggled to come up with original concepts themselves are sometimes better able to explain the work of the early pioneers than the pioneers themselves were. Larry Constantine performed the original work that led to structured design. Ed Yourdon explained Constantine's structured design work, but that explanation was still inaccessible to most readers.[30] It wasn't until Meilir Page-Jones[31] explained Yourdon's explanation that Constantine's work finally became accessible to the average practitioner.[32] Later, the concepts of structured design were absorbed into object-oriented design. And the cycle began again.

Over the long-term, knowledge that took early pioneers whole careers to master will be taught to undergraduate college students in a few semesters. It took me three and a half years to write *Code Complete.* Someday, a software developer even more "audacious" than I was will write a better book in only a few months. That is the way that lead turns slowly into gold in knowledge-intensive fields like software engineering, and that is the way it should be.

Notes

1. "ACM Fellow Profile: David Lorge Parnas," *ACM Software Engineering Notes,* May 1999, pp. 10–14.

2. For more information about these best practices, see my book *Rapid Development,* Redmond, WA: Microsoft Press, 1996.

3. Jones, Capers, *Assessment and Control of Software Risks,* Englewood Cliffs, NJ: Yourdon Press, 1994.

4. Gilb, Tom, *Principles of Software Engineering Management,* Wokingham, England: Addison-Wesley, 1988.

5. Gilb, Tom, *Software Metrics,* Cambridge, MA: Winthrop Publishers, 1977.

6. Boehm, Barry W., et al., "A Software Development Environment for Improving Productivity," *IEEE Computer,* June 1984, pp. 30–44. DeMarco, Tom, and Timothy Lister, "Programmer Performance and the Effects of the Workplace," in *Proceedings of the 8th International Conference on Software Engineering,* August 1985, pp. 268–272.

7. Risk management is much older than software itself, but software-specific papers on risk management began appearing with F. W. McFarlan, "Portfolio Approach to Information Systems," *Harvard Business Review,* September-October 1981, pp. 142–150.

8. Change control boards are much older than software itself, but software-specific books and papers on software change boards (or, more generally, software configuration management) began appearing with Edward H. Bersoff, *Proceedings of the Software Quality and Assurance Workshop,* a joint Publication of ACM *Performance Evaluation Review,* vol. 7, nos. 3 & 4, and ACM *Software Engineering Notes,* vol. 3, no. 5 (1978).

9. Brooks, Frederick P., Jr., *The Mythical Man-Month*, Reading, MA: Addison-Wesley, 1975.

10. JAD sessions were used at IBM as early as 1977, but were first reported in print in Rush, Gary, "The Fast Way to Define System Requirements," In Depth, *Computerworld*, October 7, 1985.

11. Parnas, David L., "On the Criteria to Be Used in Decomposing Systems into Modules," *Communications of the ACM*, vol. 5, no. 12, December 1972, pp. 1053–58.

12. Parnas, David L., "Designing Software for Ease of Extension and Contraction," *IEEE Transactions on Software Engineering*, v. SE-5, March 1979, pp. 128–138.

13. Various source code control tools have been around since earlier than 1980, but an early reference in print is Edward H. Bersoff, et al., *Software Configuration Management*, Englewood Cliffs, NJ: Prentice Hall, 1980.

14. Myers, Glenford J., *The Art of Software Testing*, New York: John Wiley & Sons, 1979.

15. Myers, Glenford J., *The Art of Software Testing*, New York: John Wiley & Sons, 1979.

16. Fagan, M. E., "Design and Code Inspections to Reduce Errors in Program Development," IBM Systems Journal, v. 15, no. 3, 1976, pp. 182–211.

17. Humphrey, W. S., and W. L. Sweet, *A Method for Assessing the Software Engineering Capability of Contractors*, Report CMU/SEI-87-TR-23, Pittsburgh: Software Engineering Institute, 1987.

18. Humphrey, Watts S., *Managing the Software Process*. Reading, MA, Addison-Wesley, 1989.

19. Shaw, Mary, "Prospects for an Engineering Discipline of Software," *IEEE Software*, November 1990, pp. 15f. Raghavan, Sridhar A., and Donald R. Chand, "Diffusing Software-Engineering Methods," *IEEE Software*, July 1989, pp. 81–90.

20. Rogers, Everett M., *Diffusion of Innovations*, 4th Ed., New York: The Free Press, 1995.

21. Rogers, Everett M., *Diffusion of Innovations*, 4th Ed., New York: The Free Press, 1995.

22. Moore, Geoffrey, *Crossing the Chasm*, New York: Harper Business, 1991.

23. Software-Engineering Methods," *IEEE Software*, July 1989, pp. 81–90.

24. Moore, Geoffrey, *Crossing the Chasm*, New York: Harper Business, 1991.

25. J. D. Eveland, quoted in Everett M. Rogers, *Diffusion of Innovations*, 4th Ed., New York: The Free Press, 1995. The details in this discussion about agricultural innovation are all drawn from Rogers's book.

26. Waligora, Sharon R., Linda C. Landis, Jerry T. Doland, "Closing the Loop on Improvement: Packaging Experience in the Software Engineering Laboratory,"

Proceedings of the Nineteenth Annual Software Engineering Workshop, November 30–December 1, 1994, NASA Goddard Space Flight Center, Greenbelt, MD, Document Number SEL-94-006.

27. See the SEI's Web site at www.sei.cmu.edu.

28. Agricultural worker statistics are from "Table 2, Employment by occupation, 1996 and projected 2006," in "Occupational projections to 2006," *Monthly Labor Review,* November 1997.

29. Hayes, Will, and Dave Zubrow, *Moving On Up: Data and Experience Doing CMM-Based Process Improvement,* CM/SEI-95-TR-008, August 1995.

30. Yourdon, Edward, and Constantine, Larry L., *Structured Design: Fundamentals of a Discipline of Computer Program and Systems Design,* Englewood Cliffs, NJ: Yourdon Press, 1979.

31. Page-Jones, Meilir, *The Practical Guide to Structured Systems Design,* Englewood Cliffs, NJ: Yourdon Press, 1988.

32. Constantine, Larry L., *Constantine on Peopleware,* Englewood Cliffs, NJ: Yourdon Press, 1995.

Index

Page numbers in italics refer to illustrations.

About the Author

Steve McConnell is CEO and Chief Software Engineer at Construx Software, where he writes books and articles, teaches classes, and oversees Construx's software engineering practices. He is the author of *Code Complete* (1993), *Rapid Development* (1996), and *Software Project Survival Guide* (1998). His books have twice won *Software Development* magazine's Jolt Excellence award for outstanding software development book of the year. In 1998, readers of *Software Development* magazine named Steve one of the three most influential people in the software industry along with Bill Gates and Linus Torvalds. Steve was Editor in Chief of *IEEE Software* magazine from 1998–2002. He is on the Panel of Experts that advises the Software Engineering Body of Knowledge (SWEBOK) project and is Vice Chair of the IEEE Computer Society's Professional Practices Committee.

Steve earned a bachelor's degree from Whitman College and a master's degree in software engineering from Seattle University. He lives in Bellevue, Washington.

If you have any comments or questions about this book, please contact Steve at stevemcc@construx.com or via his Web site, www.stevemcconnell.com.

Software Engineering Profession Web Site

This book has a companion Web site, www.construx.com/profession. The Web site contains materials related to the contents of this book including professional reading lists, self-study plans, descriptions of current certification and licensing initiatives, links to university software engineering programs, and pointers to many other related Web sites.

informIT

Register
Your Book

at www.awprofessional.com/register

You may be eligible to receive:

- Advance notice of forthcoming editions of the book
- Related book recommendations
- Chapter excerpts and supplements of forthcoming titles
- Information about special contests and promotions throughout the year
- Notices and reminders about author appearances, tradeshows, and online chats with special guests

Contact us

If you are interested in writing a book or reviewing manuscripts prior to publication, please write to us at:

Editorial Department
Addison-Wesley Professional
75 Arlington Street, Suite 300
Boston, MA 02116 USA
Email: AWPro@aw.com

Addison-Wesley

Visit us on the Web: http://www.awprofessional.com